The Complete **IDIOT'S** Pocket Guide to **EXCEL 5**

by Sherry Kinkoph

D0980318

alpha books

A Division of Prentice Hall Computer Publishing
201 W. 103rd Street, Indianapolis, Indiana 46290 USA

International Standard Book Number:1-56761-370-5
Library of Congress Catalog Card Number: 93-72565

95 94 93   8 7 6 5 4 3 2 1

Interpretation of the printing code: the rightmost number of the first series of numbers is the year of the book's printing; the rightmost number of the second series of numbers is the number of the book's printing. For example, a printing code of 93-1 shows that the first printing of the book occurred in 1993.

Screen reproductions in this book were created by means of the program Collage Plus from Inner Media, Inc., Hollis, NH.

Printed in the United States of America

Publisher, Marie Butler-Knight; **Associate Publisher**, Lisa A. Bucki; **Managing Editor**, Elizabeth Keaffaber; **Acquisitions Manager**, Stephen R. Poland; **Development Editor**, Kelly Oliver; **Production Editor**, Michelle Shaw; **Manuscript Editor**, San Dee Phillips; **Cover Designer**, Jean Bisesi; **Designer**, Kevin Spear; **Indexer**, Craig Small; **Production Team**, Gary Adair, Angela Bannon, Diana Bigham-Griffin, Katy Bodenmiller, Brad Chinn, Kim Cofer, Meshell Dinn, Mark Enochs, Stephanie Gregory, Jenny Kucera, Beth Rago, Marc Shecter, Greg Simsic

Contents

Introduction

Why Excel Is Better Than Your Average Calculator

You really can do just about everything with Excel 5. You can *edit* anything you want on the screen before you print it out. Need to move the second row to the end of the document? No sweat. Just click on a button. Want to **bold** a few letters or <u>underline</u> some numbers? Piece of cake. All you have to do is select the commands you want and . . . Shazam! Excel for Windows carries out your every whim.

How to Use This Book

The *Complete Idiot's Pocket Guide to Excel 5* is designed to be a friendly, easy-to-use manual for those of us who are short on time but who need to know the basics about using the new Excel release. Each lesson is brief and to the point, and is written with a conversational tone so you won't feel like you have to read each sentence 12 times to understand it.

There are special little features like tips and figures that will help you along the way. You can look at the figures to see examples of the way your screen should look when you perform certain commands or follow a set of instructions.

The tips look like this:

Read This! If you read one of these babies, you'll find some information that might turn out to be pretty helpful.

The following conventions are used to help you as you work through the lessons:

On-screen text	Text that appears on-screen appears in **bold**.
What you type	The information you type is **bold**.
What you press	The keys you press (for key combinations or commands) appear in **bold**.
Selection letters	The selection letter of each command or option is **bold** (such as File).

Acknowledgments

I'd like to thank the author of *The 10 Minute Guide to Excel 5.0*, Joe Kraynak, for teaching me practically everything I know about Excel. I'd also like to thank my ever-so-hip development editor, Kelly Oliver, who still hasn't returned my *Black Adder* tape I loaned her; and San Dee Phillips, my ever-so-clever copy editor, who could make a lot of money selling magazine subscriptions; and Michelle Shaw, my ever-so-timely production editor, for not laughing when I screwed up the figures in Lesson 8. Finally, I'd like to thank all the members of the academy for this wonderful award.

Dedication

To Ralph the wonder dog, for not eating my manuscript.

Lesson 1

Let's Open This Baby and Take It for a Spin

How Do You Start This Thing?

First of all, you have to know where to find the Excelerator. Get it? Excel-erator! Ha, ha, ha. Okay, enough of that. Make sure your computer and monitor are turned on, in case you computer rookies out there haven't thought of that yet. Before you can even think about starting Microsoft Excel, you have to start Windows. That's right, you have to run another program before you can run the program you really want to run—welcome to the world of computers.

Locate the glaring DOS prompt, which looks like C:> or C:\>, type **WIN** and then press **Enter**. If your computer is set up to run Windows as soon as you turn it on, you won't have a DOS prompt, so you won't have to worry about all of this.

Bad command or filename! If your computer displays this message, try typing **CD\WINDOWS**. Press **Enter**, and then type **WIN** again. If your computer isn't set up to start Windows automatically when it's turned on, you'll have to perform this routine every time. Or if you're feeling particularly daring, you can edit your AUTOEXEC.BAT file to include the Windows directory in your path statement. Since that's a DOS thing, you'll have to check your DOS manual to figure out how. Bummer.

After you've started Windows, the Windows Program Manager screen will appear. To start Excel for Windows, you have to find the Microsoft Office icon on the Windows Program Manager screen. An *icon* is a little graphical representation of the program. (If your Program Manager screen isn't showing, hold down the **Alt** key, and press **Esc** one or more times until it is displayed.)

When you find the Microsoft Office program group icon, move the mouse pointer directly on top of the icon. Then rapidly press and release the left mouse button twice (this is called *double-clicking*). If you're using the keyboard, press **Ctrl+Tab** until the icon is highlighted (or suddenly has a solid bar around the name), and then press **Enter**. ("Press **Ctrl+Tab**" means you should hold down the **Ctrl** key while pressing the **Tab** key, and then release both keys. The technical name for this little routine is a *keystroke combination*, or *shortcut key*. Are you impressed?)

This should open up the Microsoft Office program group window (whew, what a mouthful) as shown in Figure 1.1. And what the heck is a program group window? It's just another window on your screen that has icons from the same program in it.

Now locate the Microsoft Excel icon. Start Excel by selecting the Microsoft Excel icon, using either your mouse or keyboard. Don't panic, I'm going to tell you how. If you are using the mouse, position the mouse pointer on the Microsoft Excel icon, then double-click (you learned how to do this earlier). If you are using the keyboard, use the arrow keys to move the highlight to the Microsoft Excel icon, and then press **Enter**.

Look! It's the Windows
Program Manager screen!

This is the title bar with
the title of the window in it.

Here's the Microsoft
Office program group
window opened up.

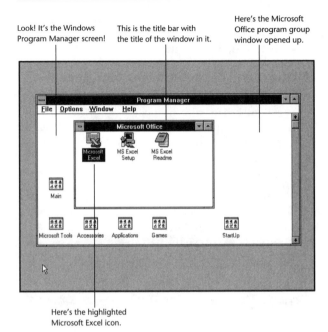

Here's the highlighted
Microsoft Excel icon.

Figure 1.1 *The Windows Program Manager screen. Ooh-la-la.*

Hey, I Don't Have an Icon—I Am Iconless! If you can't find the icon, you probably haven't installed Excel yet. Turn to the back of this book for installation instructions. Or perhaps during installation you designated another program group window to put it in other than the default Microsoft Office group. In this case, you'll have to look among the other program group windows on your Program Manager screen. Hypnosis might also help you remember where you installed it.

When Excel starts, the opening screen with copyright notices appears, and then you will see the main screen, as shown in Figure 1.2.

What's All This Stuff on the Screen?

Think of the Microsoft Excel screen as a big, blank workbook full of worksheet pages waiting to be typed on. The area surrounding the workbook shows you all sorts of nifty little things. You can look at Figure 1.2 to see where they are, then look at the following list to see what they are (hope you don't mind a little eyeball workout):

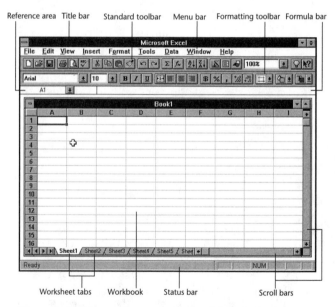

Figure 1.2 Feast your eyes on the Excel for Windows screen.

☞ The *title bar* tells you the program name and the name of the document you're working on.

☞ The *menu bar* contains—surprisingly enough—menus.

☞ The *Standard toolbar* has buttons that you can select to perform common editing tasks (as opposed to noble editing tasks, I guess). One hitch: you must have a mouse to use the toolbar.

☞ The *Formatting toolbar* has buttons you can use to select fonts, font sizes, and other commands that affect the look of your text.

☞ The *Formula bar* displays data you enter, such as mathematical formulas.

☞ The *workbook* contains worksheets that you can use to enter data or formulate figures. A worksheet is made up of cells formed by intersecting rows and columns. The tabs at the bottom of the workbook window let you flip through the worksheets.

☞ You can use *scroll bars* to move around your document with the mouse.

☞ The *status bar* displays information about your document.

So, What's a Workbook?

Good question. In earlier versions of Excel, a single worksheet appeared on your screen whenever you started the program. With the new and improved Excel 5.0, you get 16 worksheets arranged into a workbook file. See those little tabs at the bottom of Figure 1.2? Each one is a single worksheet. And why do you have 16 worksheets in a workbook file, you may ask? That's just the default number the fine programmers at Excel picked out. Maybe they think you've got a lot of work to do, or something.

So just what is a worksheet, then? Well, it's a page in a workbook that can be used to enter data, perform calculations, organize information, and more. Worksheets look like grids, with intersecting columns and rows that form little boxes, called *cells*. Worksheets are arranged in workbook files. When you first start the Excel program, there are 16 worksheets in a workbook file. But you can change this number, adding or deleting worksheets to suit your needs. Confused? Don't worry, this will all be clear to you in the lessons to come. I promise.

Careful Where You Point That Thing: A Word to New Mouse Users

You can use Excel for Windows without a mouse, but having one makes everything faster and easier. If you aren't familiar with the mouse, peruse the next few paragraphs to get a feel for it.

The *mouse pointer* is an arrow, or other symbol, on the screen that moves as you move the mouse on your desk. The shape of the mouse pointer varies depending on what Excel is doing at the moment. For example, an arrow is the default pointer shape and means that you can perform normal operations. A mouse pointer shaped like an hourglass means that Excel is busy carrying out an operation. You have to wait until the pointer changes back to an arrow or other symbol before you can do anything.

There are several important mouse terms that you should become familiar with before going any further:

Point   Move the mouse pointer to a specific screen location.

Click   Quickly press and release the left mouse button.

Double-click   Quickly press and release the left mouse button twice.

Drag   Move the mouse while holding the left button down.

Careful What You Press: Equal Time for Keyboard Users

Just so you keyboard people don't feel left out, here are a few pointers to using the keyboard to move around.

Tip number one: *arrow keys*. Yup, those handy arrow keys on your keyboard are an excellent mode of transportation for you. Use them when you can.

Tip number two: *shortcut keys*. You'll learn more about these in Lesson 3.

Tip number three: you won't go far without your trusty **Enter** key. Keep it nearby. There—that's all.

Next, I'm going to show you some basic Windows navigational skills. Hang onto your seats, this will be more thrilling than a ride at Disneyland.

Lesson 2

Looking Through Your Windows

Your Basic Windows Parts, Plus Labor

One great thing about Windows programs is that they all share a common user interface. Yikes, what's that mean? Quite simply, all Windows programs look pretty much the same. Oh sure, the details and functions vary from program to program, but when you learn the basic parts of a Windows window you will be able to recognize those parts in every Windows program, including Excel. Take a look at the parts of the Excel program window shown in Figure 2.1.

Program window   Think of this as the big picture window of the program. This window frames the tools, menus, and the worksheet area.

Workbook window   This area of the screen frames the controls and information for the worksheets you're working on. You can have several workbook windows open at the same time, in case you wanted to know that.

Title bar   There are two of these guys. One displays the title of the program, and the other displays the name of the current workbook you're working on.

Menu bar   You'll see the names of the different menus for Excel located on the menu bar. These menus contain commands that can be used to build your worksheets.

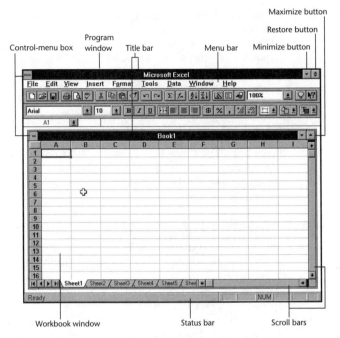

Figure 2.1 *Fascinating window parts that you'll want to know about.*

Control-menu box Click on this button to display a menu with commands for resizing, closing, and moving windows.

Minimize button Clicking on this button will reduce the window to an icon at the bottom of your screen.

Maximize button And clicking on this button will increase the size of your window to fill the screen.

Restore button Click on this button to restore the window to its previous size.

Scroll bars Gee, there are so many bars around here, it's beginning to look like a red-light district! You use the scroll bars to display different sections of your worksheet. You can click on the arrows in the scroll bars to move up or down, right or left, or you can drag the scroll box up and down like an elevator car. You'll find scroll bars located along the right side and the bottom of the worksheet window.

Status bar The lowly bar at the very bottom of your window is the status bar. It displays information about the worksheet or about the commands you are using.

Custom-Size Your Windows

What do you do if you want a different sized window? Resize it. You can adjust the size of any window by using the mouse or the keyboard. To resize a window using the mouse, just move the mouse pointer to the window edge you want to resize. When you've placed the mouse pointer over the window border, the pointer will become a double-headed arrow. (How do they make it do that?) Then press and hold the left mouse button and drag the window border to a new location. When you've sized the window the way you want it, let go of the left mouse button.

Two Sides at Once Looking for a faster way to resize? You can move both the horizontal and vertical borders at the same time if you place the mouse pointer at a corner. When the pointer becomes a double-headed arrow, press and drag the mouse. The windows corner will move, dragging both borders with it. What technology, huh?

For those of you who insist upon using your keyboards, you can resize your window with the Control menu. (You'll learn more about menus in the next lesson.) Open the Control menu by pressing **Alt+Spacebar**. When the Control menu is displayed, press **S**. Depending on which direction you want to go, press the arrow keys to select the appropriate border, then continue pressing the arrow keys to resize the window. When it's the size you want, press **Enter**. Now wasn't that amazing?

What's a Control-Menu Box?   It's the little, tiny box with a dash in it. You'll find it in the upper left corner of your workbook or your screen. (I pointed one out for you in Figure 2.1.) If you click on the Control-menu box, or press **Alt+Spacebar** to open the Control menu for the program window or **Alt+ –** to open the Control menu for the workbook window, it will open to reveal a menu of commands for resizing, closing, and moving the program window. If you double-click on it, you'll exit the program.

You can resize your workbook window the same way, except use **Alt+ –** to open the workbook Control menu.

Maximize, Minimize, Economize

If you've been playing around with resizing your windows, you may be interested in knowing how to get them back to their original size. Or maybe you're just curious about those little arrow buttons in the upper right corner of your screen. In either case, I'm going to tell you how to minimize, maximize, and restore your windows.

If you're using the mouse, you can click on the **Minimize** button (the downward-pointing arrow shown in Figure 2.1) to reduce your window into the size of an icon. If you're using the keyboard, press **Ctrl+F9**. To get the icon back to it's original state, double-click on the icon, or press **Ctrl+F5**.

Use the **Maximize** button to make your window fill the entire screen. Click the upward-pointing arrow shown in Figure 2.1, or press **Ctrl+F10**. If the button shows a double-headed arrow, that means the window is maximized to its fullest state. Click on the double-headed button, known as the **Restore** button, to reduce the size of your window. Yes, there's a keyboard shortcut: press **Ctrl+F5**.

Move It or Lose It

You can also move your windows around. Click on the title bar, hold down the left mouse button, drag the window where you want it to go, then let go of the mouse button. You can use the keyboard, but you have to open the Control menu. Press **Alt+Spacebar**, then select Move from the menu list by pressing **M** (or you can press **Ctrl+F7**). When the pointer becomes a four-headed arrow, use the keyboard arrow keys to move the entire window to a new location. When you've got it where you want it, press **Enter**.

Now that you know how to recognize a Windows screen from across the room, let's move on to the drama of Excel's emergency help system.

Lesson 3

Help! Excel's Answer to 911

How Do I Get Help When I'm in a Jam?

Excel for Windows has a convenient system for helping you through rough spots. It's called, appropriately, *Help*. It's like a life preserver when you're sinking in your own worksheet confusion. One way to access the help system is through the Help menu. As you can see in Figure 3.1, the Help pull-down menu has many commands to choose from.

Figure 3.1   *The Help menu—designed to float in water.*

- ☞ Help Contents calls up the main help system table of contents.
- ☞ The Search for Help on command brings up a dialog box in which you can enter specific information you want to look up.
- ☞ The Index provides an alphabetical listing of Help topics and words. You can scroll through the list, or select an alphabet letter for a more precise search.

- ☞ The Quick Preview and the Examples and Demos commands will bring up tutorials and examples of Excel tasks and functions.

- ☞ Lotus 1-2-3 is an interpreter that assists Lotus users in understanding Excel commands.

- ☞ Multiplan does the same thing as Lotus 1-2-3, except it assists Multiplan users instead.

- ☞ The Technical Support option reveals nitty-gritty information about what to do when things go wrong. This can really come in handy.

- ☞ Lastly, the About Microsoft Excel option displays a box with brief information about the Excel program. The key word here is "brief." You'll find the program version and memory availability listed here.

The major Help commands are explained next. Please refer to your program documentation if you would like detailed information on the other parts of the Help menu.

Have No Fear, Help Contents Is Here

The Help Contents is command central for the help system. Using the Contents, you can easily locate help information on any topic. To display the opening page of the contents, select Help Contents, or press **F1** while working in your document. The Help window is initially displayed as a window overlapping your worksheet screen, as shown in Figure 3.2.

Don't Forget About the Nifty Help Tool There's a nifty Help tool located on your Standard toolbar. It looks like a question mark. When you click on the button, your mouse pointer becomes a question mark icon. Position the icon over the item on your screen that you want help with, and then click on the left mouse button. You can also double-click on the button to search for a Help topic.

Command buttons

Control-menu box   The Help menu bar

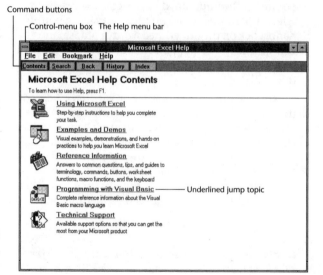

Figure 3.2 The Help window displaying Excel Help Contents.

Flipping Through Your Help Contents

The Help window has five command buttons at the top: Contents, Search, Back, History, and Index (see Figure 3.2). Use these buttons to move around the help system. To select a button, click on it with the mouse, or press **Alt+***n*, where *n* is the underlined letter in the button name. Like other commands, if a button is grayed, you can't select it.

In the help system, certain terms and phrases are underlined and displayed in a different color. A solid underline indicates a *jump topic*. Move the mouse pointer to the underlined word or phrase you want to select. When the mouse pointer looks like a pointing hand, click on the underlined word or phrase, and you will go directly to help information on that topic (it really is like jumping, which explains the *jump* part of the name).

A dotted underline under a word or phrase tells you that you can look at a definition of that term. When the mouse pointer looks like a pointing hand, you can click on the word or phrase to see a definition. Click on the button again to make the definition disappear. You can also press **Tab** or **Shift+Tab** to move a highlight bar between underlined terms, and then hold down the **Enter** key to see the definition.

Don't Laugh, Help Is Sensitive   The Excel for Windows help system is *context-sensitive*. This means that if you are selecting a menu command or entering information in a dialog box, pressing **F1** will automatically display help information on your current task. Pretty handy, eh?

Lesson 4

Ordering from Menus

Bring Me a Menu, Please

Did you ever think that using Excel would be the equivalent of a fine-dining experience? Well it's not, except for the use of menus. There are so many different commands you can give with Excel for Windows that they have to be organized somehow. That's where *menus* come in. When you select a menu, its commands are displayed and you can choose one.

Excel has two types of menus, the main menu and the pull-down menu. The *main menu* is displayed in the *menu bar*, on the second line of the screen. Here, you'll find nine tantalizing and delectable menu types to choose from. A *pull-down menu* is a list of commands associated with each choice on the main menu. When you choose a menu from the main menu, thwap! It drops down like a window shade, except without that noise.

A pull-down menu is shown in Figure 4.1. Notice that the status bar (the bottom line on the screen) displays a brief description of the currently highlighted menu command. (The highlighted menu appears in a different color.) In Figure 4.1, for example, the Edit Copy command is highlighted. The status bar at the bottom of the screen tells you that this command will **Copy selected cells to the Clipboard**.

Pull-down menu   Highlight bar   Shortcut key   Menu bar

Selection letter   Grayed text   Ellipsis   Sub-menu arrows   Status bar

Figure 4.1 *Excel menus. Funny, there are no prices on these menus—that means everything's going to be really expensive.*

How to Read Your Menu

If you look closely at the pull-down menus (such as the one shown in Figure 4.1), you will notice that some of the commands look a little different and some have keystroke combinations after them. (Keystroke combinations tell you to push two or more keys at once.) The styles won't mean anything to you until you know what they are, but if you know what they mean they can help you out a lot.

☛ If a command has a different-colored bar around it, that means it's highlighted or selected. This is called a *highlight bar*. (Don't you find it rather peculiar that the word "bar" keeps popping up with the use of this program? I wonder what that means?)

☛ A keystroke combination listed after a command is called a *shortcut key*. It's a way to choose the command from the keyboard without using the whole menu system. For example, the shortcut key for the Edit Copy command is **Ctrl+C**. Of course, you have to memorize these so you won't have to keep pulling down menus to find out what the shortcut keys are.

☛ An ellipsis (the three dot thingy) following a command tells you that a dialog box will pop up when you select the command. (You'll learn about dialog boxes in Lesson 5. Wow, something to look forward to.)

☛ An underlined letter in a menu command indicates the key that you can press to select the command when the menu is displayed. For example, when the Edit menu is displayed, press **C** to select Copy. (The technical name for the underlined letter is *selection letter*, in case you wanted to know but were afraid to ask.) Selection letters are just another way to choose menu commands. Variety is the spice of life, you know.

☛ If a command has an arrow next to it, that means a sub-menu will be displayed when you select the command. Quite simply, there's just more menu to look at.

☛ If a command is grayed, it means you can't select it. You can select it only under certain conditions, and those conditions aren't happening right now. So don't even think about selecting it.

How Do I Order from These Fancy Menus?

Before you select a command, you have to select a menu. (Stands to reason, doesn't it?) If you're using a mouse, just click on the menu name. Simple enough. If you're using the keyboard, press **F10** to activate the menu bar, and then press the underlined letter of the menu. After you've activated the menu bar, you can also move to the menu using the arrow keys, and press **Enter**. Or you can hold down the **Alt** key and press the selection letter of the menu name. (Great, another hundred ways to do one simple thing—a typical computer programming ploy.)

To select a command from a pull-down menu with the mouse, click on it. With the keyboard, press the underlined selection letter in the command, or move to the menu item you want using the arrow keys, and then press **Enter**. If you mess up, you can cancel your most recent choice by pressing **Esc**. To get out of the menu entirely, click anywhere outside the menu.

From here on out, I'm going to shorten these instructions for selecting commands. For example, if I tell you to "select File New," you should select the File menu and then select New from the File menu commands. The decision to make the selection with the mouse or keyboard is completely up to you. (What freedom!)

Now that you've messed around with menus, you're ready to carry on some dialog with the dialog boxes.

Lesson 5

Bossing Your Computer Around with Dialog Boxes

Those Demanding Dialog Boxes

When Excel needs to force more information out of you before it can carry out a command, a *dialog box* pops up. Dialog boxes can contain many components but usually contain only a few. Figure 5.1 shows a typical dialog box.

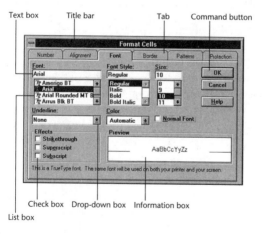

Figure 5.1   Components of a dialog box.

A *dotted outline* or *highlight bar* indicates the current dialog box item selected.

The *title bar* tells you which dialog box you're looking at.

Some dialog boxes arrange information in little *tab* folders that you can flip through to make selections.

A *text box* is used to type in specific information.

A *list box* displays a list of items you can choose from. If the list is too big to display at one time, a vertical scroll bar lets you scroll up or down the list.

A *drop-down box* is similar to a list box, but displays only a single item unless it is opened. Drop-down boxes always have arrows by them.

An *information box* displays information about the item selected in the list box.

Check boxes turn options on (an **X** is displayed) or off (no **X** is displayed), like a light switch. One or more check box options in a group can be on at a time.

Option buttons also turn options on or off with a circular bullet, but, unlike check boxes, only one option button in a group may be on at a time. (Not shown in Figure 5.1.)

The *command buttons* either confirm or cancel the dialog box. They usually say **OK** or **Cancel**. Sometimes, selecting them will display another dialog box or a drop-down menu list.

Making Your Own Demands in Dialog Boxes

So, how do you converse with these dialog boxes, you may ask? To move around and make selections in the dialog box with the mouse, just click on whatever you want to select. If it's a tab dialog box (one with those tab folders in it), you can click on the tab to bring the information to the front of the dialog box. If it's an option button or a check box, clicking on it will turn it on or off, or *toggle* it. If it's a drop-down box, click on the adjacent arrow to make the list drop down, and then click on the item you want. When a text box is selected, the editing position is indicated by a blinking vertical cursor. Any new text you type will be entered at the cursor position. Got all that?

For you keyboard users out there, you'll find a few different ways you can move around in a dialog box. To move forward or backward between items and groups of items, press **Tab** or **Shift+Tab**.

To move directly to a dialog box item and to display a drop-down list, press **Alt+***n*, where *n* is the letter underlined in the item's name. Pretty groovy, eh? To select an item within a group, use the arrow keys. To select an item in a drop-down box or list box, use the ↓, ↑, Home, End, PgUp, and PgDn keys to scroll among the items in the box. To close a drop-down box, press **Alt+↑**. To toggle a check box or option button on and off, select it, and then press the **Spacebar**. To bring a different tab to the front of the dialog box, press **Ctrl+Alt+**left or right arrow key.

To cancel the dialog box without executing the command and also cancel any options you've entered in the box, select the **Cancel** button and press **Enter**, or press **Esc**. To close the dialog box without executing the command, while keeping any option changes you've made, select the **Close** button, and press **Enter**. To confirm the dialog box options and execute the command, press **Enter**. Whew, we're really zipping through this stuff.

Get Me Out of This Box!   If you ever need to exit a dialog box, click on the **Close** or **Cancel** button, or press **Esc**. You can also double-click on the *Control-menu box*. That's the little box in the upper-left corner of the dialog box with a dash-thing in it.

Enough dialog about the dialog boxes. Next, I'll explain what those toolbar things are all about.

Lesson 6

Meet Mr. Toolbar

They Look Like Buttons to Me

As you learned in Lesson 1, the bar below the menu bar is called the Standard toolbar, and the bar below that is the Formatting toolbar. At this point, you may be thinking, Just what is a toolbar anyway? Why do these tools look like buttons? Why would I need tools when I've got an expensive computer to do everything for me? If I wanted tools, I'd go to Sears, especially if they're having a Craftsman sale.

A *toolbar* contains buttons that represent frequently used commands—shortcuts. All you have to do to use a toolbar button is click on it. You'll quickly find that clicking on a toolbar button is quicker and more convenient than entering the entire command sequence. (Sorry keyboard users, you can only select the buttons with the mouse. How cruel.)

As for why they call it a toolbar, it's probably because, like tools, these buttons are mighty handy to use and are in easy reach. (Just be grateful you don't have to wear them in a leather belt slung around your waist.) Figure 6.1 has the Standard and Formatting toolbars pointed out for you.

When you first start Excel, the Standard and Formatting toolbars will automatically appear on your screen. The Standard toolbar allows you to execute the most often used menu commands. Want to know what those are? You'll find a table on the inside front cover of this book detailing the commands. On the other hand, the Formatting toolbar has a whole other set of tools you can use to make your text look good.

(That's what formatting is, by the way, making your text look good.) You'll find a table on the inside back cover of this book detailing what those are.

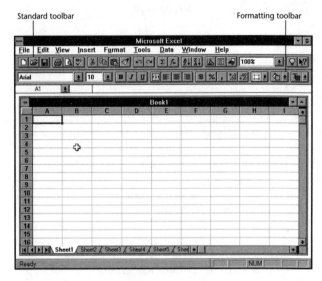

Figure 6.1 *The Excel default toolbars—the Standard toolbar and the Formatting toolbar.*

However, if you lose this book or are just too tired to turn to the front or back covers, there's another way you can find out what a toolbar button does. Move your mouse pointer over the button you want to know about, but don't click. A tiny ToolTip box will appear next to the button revealing the name of the tool. That's not all—look down at the status bar at the bottom of your screen. You'll find a brief description of what the tool does. Pretty slick, huh?

Use the Nifty Help Tool At the very end of the Standard toolbar is a button with a question mark on it—that's the Help tool. When you click on it, your mouse pointer becomes a question mark. Move the pointer to any tool or part of the screen that you want help with, click the mouse button, and help information will appear.

Hiding (and Displaying) Your Toolbar

When you get tired of looking at your toolbars, here's how to make them disappear. (You can also use these same steps to display a toolbar.) Select View Toolbars. Click on the View menu, or press **Alt+V**. Then click on Toolbars, or press **T**. When the Show Toolbars dialog box appears, select the particular toolbar you want to hide or display.

Those little check boxes next to the toolbar names will indicate whether the toolbar is selected or not. If there's an X in the box, the toolbar will appear on your screen. If there's no X in the box, that toolbar is not displayed. (Look at Figure 6.2 to see the Toolbars dialog box.) When you've made your selection, click on **OK** or press **Enter**.

Look! There's More of Them! In case you hadn't noticed, the Toolbars dialog reveals a plethora of toolbars you can use. Excel has a total of thirteen toolbars, including the default toolbars you just learned about. They all have different uses, and I'd love to tell you about each one, but there's not enough room in this book. But a good way to learn is to try them out!

Figure 6.2 *The Toolbars dialog box—showcase for the many fine Excel toolbars.*

Another way to hide or display a toolbar is to move the mouse pointer anywhere inside a toolbar and click the right mouse button. This will display the Toolbars shortcut menu. Click on a toolbar name to turn it on or off.

I Want This Toolbar Out of My Way!

Not only can you display all of these toolbars in your work area, you can also move and resize the toolbars to suit your taste. But a word of warning, try not to get too many on your screen at the same time or you won't have any room to work. Figure 6.3 shows a worksheet with four toolbars in various areas.

When a toolbar is initially displayed, it is placed at the top or bottom of the work area. But you don't have to keep it there. You can move it any time. Move your mouse pointer to an open space on the toolbar, press the left mouse button and drag the toolbar to a new location. If you drag it to the top or bottom edge of your worksheet, the toolbar remains horizontal. If you move the toolbar away from the top or bottom edge, it becomes a floating toolbar.

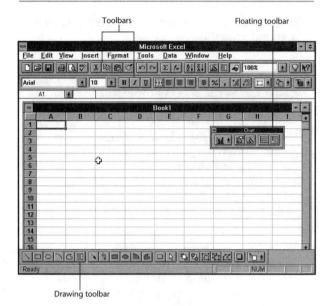

Figure 6.3 *An Excel worksheet displaying four toolbars.*

The Mysterious Floating Toolbar Any toolbars that are not positioned at the top or bottom edge of your window are called *floating toolbars*. (I've pointed one out for you in Figure 6.3.) They act like little windows, complete with Control-menu boxes and title bars. To quickly move a floating toolbar to the top of the screen, double-click on its title bar.

You can resize a toolbar by grabbing it by the edge with the mouse pointer, like any window, and dragging that edge to the new size. After a toolbar has been resized, the tools within it will be rearranged to accommodate the new size.

Can I Change the Way My Toolbars Look? Sure. You can modify a toolbar to suit your needs, or create your very own toolbar. To customize a toolbar, select **V**iew **T**oolbar. When the Toolbars dialog box appears, type in the name for your new toolbar, and then click on the **New** button or press **Alt+N**. Excel will create a new floating toolbar and display the Customize dialog box. Drag the desired buttons onto the new toolbar. When you're finished, select **Close**.

Now that you know practically everything you ever needed to know about toolbars, and then some, let's move on to learning everything you ever wanted to know, and then some, about moving around in worksheets.

Lesson 7

Windows Aerobics

How Do You Move Around in Here?

Okay. So you're looking at your Excel screen and thinking "Hey, how do I move around in this workbook thing?" You can move around in an Excel workbook by using the mouse or the keyboard. I personally prefer the mouse, it seems to require less thinking—you just grab it and go. If you use the keyboard, you'll have to remember what keys to press and what commands they activate. Sounds like a lot of trouble to me. But maybe you like a lot of trouble. Whatever.

If you were paying any attention at all in Lesson 1, you learned that workbooks are comprised of worksheets, and worksheets are comprised of columns and rows. Where a column and row intersect, it forms a box called a *cell*. To move around from cell to cell, point your mouse pointer to the cell and click. The cell you click on becomes highlighted, or surrounded by a dark line (called a *Selector*). That means the cell is *active* and is ready for you to type in numbers or text. Figure 7.1 shows an active cell.

Using the keyboard to move around is a little more complicated. Lucky for you, I've included this handy chart of key combinations you can use. Take a look at Table 7.1 on the next page.

Table 7.1   Worksheet Navigation Keys

Key	Function
↑	Moves one cell up
↓	Moves one cell down
←	Moves one cell left
→	Moves one cell right
PgUp	Moves one screen up
PgDn	Moves one screen down
Ctrl+PgUp	Moves to the previous sheet
Ctrl+PgDn	Moves to the next sheet
End+ any arrow key	Moves in the indicated direction, to the last cell with data
Ctrl+End	Moves to the last cell in the worksheet
Ctrl+Home	Moves to the first cell in the worksheet

Scrolling Along the Boulevard

Another way to get around your workbooks is to use those wonderful scroll bar thingys. They're located on the bottom and right sides of the worksheet (see Figure 7.1). You'll find scroll bars are an easy way to move quickly around a large worksheet filled with data.

To scroll along your worksheet, point your mouse pointer on the arrow that's going in the direction you need to go. Then press the left mouse button to start moving. Careful, these scroll bars can really pick up steam. When you've reached the area of your screen where you want to stop, let go of the mouse button.

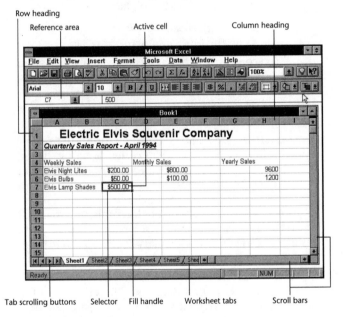

Figure 7.1 *Here's an active cell—a highlighted square where a row and column intersect.*

You can scroll in smaller increments by just clicking the scroll arrows. You can scroll in larger increments by dragging the scroll box. Or you can try these scroll bar tips:

To scroll through one column, click on the right arrow located on the horizontal scroll bar.

To scroll through one row, click on the down arrow located on the vertical scroll bar.

To scroll one screen up or down, click between the arrows on the vertical scroll bar.

To scroll one screen left or right, click between the arrows on the horizontal scroll bar.

You can scroll through the different worksheets in a workbook by clicking on the tab scrolling buttons, shown in Figure 7.1.

Where Am I?

Sometimes, you can get lost among all of your worksheet cells. Unless you've left a trail of bread crumbs on your screen, it's a good idea to learn about cell references, or names. Each cell is identified with a reference, depending on which row or column it's in. These worksheets are laid out like grids, and each cell in the grid has a name. Guess what the top left cell's name is? If you said A1, smarty-pants, you were right.

Columns are labeled with alphabet letters, and rows are labeled with numbers. Cell names always reference the column letter first, then the row number. So a cell named A1 is the top left cell in a worksheet. If you ever get confused, look at the reference area below the menu bar. This is kind of like a "you-are-here" marker. Notice where the highlighted cell is in Figure 7.1? It's in column C, row 7. The reference area confirms this, it says **C7**. How about that? You won't need that compass after all.

Tip

Get Out of My Way—I Know Where I'm Going You can move to a specific cell in the worksheet by selecting the **G**o To command on the **E**dit menu. In the **R**eference box, type the name of the cell you would like to move to (for example, type **G12**), and then click on **OK**, or press **Enter**.

Feel like exercising a bit more? Good, because in the next lesson, you'll learn all about working out with workbooks.

Lesson 8

Workbook Workouts: Open, Close, Open, Close

Work Up a Sweat, Open a Workbook

That last lesson was just a mild warm-up compared to this one. You're going to get a real workout now. Put down that bag of chips and listen up. There are a few basics you need to know about working with workbooks, also known as *files* or *documents*. This lesson will show you how to open a workbook file, find a workbook you've already made, close a file, and open more than one workbook at the same time.

Anytime you want to open a new workbook, use the File New command. Open the File menu, and select the New command. A new workbook will open on-screen with a default name in the title bar, such as **BOOK1**, as shown in Figure 8.1.

Toolbar Shortcut! Here's your chance to use a toolbar button. To open a new workbook, simply click on the **New Workbook** tool on the Standard toolbar. (I pointed this out for you in Figure 8.1.)

Low Impact Workout: Opening an Existing Workbook

If you've already got some workbooks created and saved, you'll probably want to open them up again. Why? To admire your Excel worksheet-building prowess, of course. Or perhaps you need to go back in and change a few things.

New Workbook button

Open button Default name

Figure 8.1 *Use the New command to open a new workbook.*

To open an existing workbook, use the File Open command. Pull down the File menu, and select **Open**. The Open dialog box shown in Figure 8.2 will appear. Select the name of the file you're looking for from the File Name list. Do this by clicking on the file name, or typing the name into the text box. (If you can't see the name of the file in the displayed list, use the scroll bar to scroll through the list.) To actually open the file, click on **OK**, or press **Enter**.

Another Shortcut! To quickly display the Open dialog box, click on the **Open** button on the Standard toolbar. (I pointed this one out for you in Figure 8.1.)

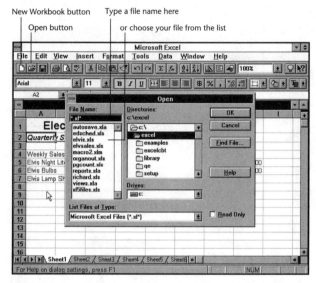

Figure 8.2   Oooh—The Open dialog box.

I Have No Idea Where My File Is

If you're suffering from temporary amnesia and can't remember the name of the file you want to retrieve, use the Find File button in the Open dialog box to find it. When you select Find File, the Search dialog box is displayed. Under the Search For options, select the File Name type you are looking for, such as Excel documents (*.xl*). (Those *'s stand for wild cards— any character goes!) Then type in the location of the search, such as **C:\EXCEL** (**C:** stands for drive C, **EXCEL** is the Excel for Windows directory). Select **OK**, and Excel searches the disk/directory specified for files that match the search criteria. Then the dialog box shown in Figure 8.3 is displayed.

File list   Preview area

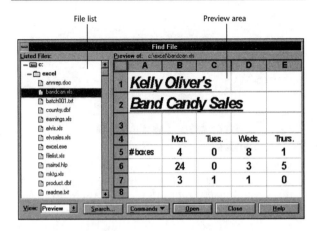

Figure 8.3 *The Find File dialog box.*

If you see your file in the Listed Files list box, double-click on it, or move down to it using the arrow keys, and press **Enter**. If you're not sure what your file's name is, you can look at the Preview area to see the contents of each file as it's highlighted in the file list. Pretty nifty!

Stop Sweating, Close a Workbook

To close a workbook, use the File Close command. This command will remove the workbook from the screen. Pull down the File menu, and choose Close, or press **Alt+F** and then the letter C. If you haven't saved the workbook yet, a box will pop up on-screen asking you to do so. Unless you never want to see that workbook or those workbook changes again, it's a good idea to save your data. (You'll learn about saving files in Lesson 12.)

In a Hurry?   To quickly close a worksheet, double-click on the **Control** button located in the upper-left corner.

Two, Count 'Em, Two Open Workbooks

Sometimes, you may want to have more than one workbook open at a time. Why? Because you might want to flip back and forth between them, or maybe you want to copy text from one to the other. There are lots of good reasons, trust me. Now, let me show you how. First, you should start out with one workbook open on your screen. Got that? Next, open another workbook—without closing or exiting the first one. Did you do that? Good, now you've got two open workbooks.

Slow Down! You're Going Too Fast   Sorry. I'm just taking it for granted that you remember how to open a workbook since you just read about it earlier in this lesson. To open an existing workbook, select File Open, and choose the workbook file you want from the list. If you're opening a new workbook file, just click on the **New Workbook** button on the Standard toolbar.

When you have multiple workbooks open at one time, only one of them can be active, or in use at a given moment. That makes sense. The active workbook is displayed on-screen and is the only one affected by editing commands. You can have many workbooks open at the same time (based on their size and your computer's memory), and you can switch between them at will. Take a moment to think of all the power you have at your fingertips. Absolutely incredible!

Now try switching between workbooks. Select the Window menu, which lists all open workbooks. (A check mark is next to the name of the currently active workbook, as shown in Figure 8.4.) Select the workbook name to make active. You can either click on the workbook name with the mouse or press the key corresponding to the number listed next to the name on the menu. The selected workbook becomes active and is displayed on-screen.

Figure 8.4 *The Window menu with a check mark next to the active workbook name.*

How Can You Tell It's Active? If a workbook is active, its title bar is highlighted with a solid color bar. If a worksheet is active, its tab appears to be in front of the other worksheet tabs. Now don't ask me again.

Next Please! Have you got more than two workbooks open? To cycle to the next open workbook, press **Ctrl+F6**. If that's not the one you want, press **Ctrl+F6** again until you get to the right one.

I'm Seeing Double

There may come a day when you will want to have two or more open documents visible on-screen at the same time. To do so, select Window Arrange, and then select Tiled or Cascade from the next dialog box. Excel displays each open workbook in its own window in the work area. For example, Figure 8.5 shows two workbooks displayed in the work area in the Tiled format. Note that each workbook window has its own title bar that displays the workbook name.

The active document is indicated by a dark background in the title bar and a dark border. In Figure 8.5, **ELVSALES.XLS** is active. To make a different workbook window active, click anywhere in the window with the mouse. You can also press **Ctrl+F6** one or more times to cycle between windows, or use the Window command as described earlier in this lesson.

I've Had It with This Multiple Document Display To return to a full-screen display of a single workbook, make the workbook you want active, then maximize the window. (Remember that lesson about minimizing and maximizing windows? If you've forgotten, go back to Lesson 2, do not pass Go or collect $200.)

The active workbook has a highlighted title bar.

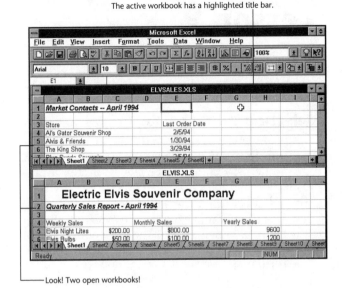

Look! Two open workbooks!

Figure 8.5 *Multiple workbooks displayed with Window Arrange.*

In the next lesson, we'll work on developing good worksheet muscle tone. Isn't this fun?

Lesson 9

Tone Up Your Worksheet Muscles

Selecting Worksheets

All right, if you've survived the workbook files calisthenics in Lesson 8, you're ready to wind down with worksheet stretching. That includes selecting, inserting, deleting, and copying worksheets. Pay attention.

To select a worksheet, just click on its tab. To select several neighboring worksheets (worksheets that are next to each other), click on the first worksheet in the group and then hold down the **Shift** key while clicking on the last worksheet. Careful, don't pull a muscle.

To select several non-neighboring worksheets (worksheets that aren't next to each other), hold down the **Ctrl** key, and click on each worksheet. If you goof up and select the wrong one, just press the **Ctrl** key again while you're clicking the worksheet's tab to unselect it.

Give Me More Worksheets

You can add new worksheets anywhere in your workbook. To insert a new worksheet in a workbook, select the worksheet that follows where you want a new worksheet to go. For example, if you select Sheet6, the new worksheet will be inserted before Sheet6. (To really confuse you, the new worksheet you insert is given the next available default name. So if your workbook has sixteen worksheets and you add another, it's named Sheet17—even though you make it appear before Sheet6. Got that?)

Next, open the Insert menu, and select Worksheet. Excel inserts the new worksheet. Wasn't that easy?

Secret Shortcut Menu Hey—this tip is better than a decoder ring! If you click the right mouse button while your mouse pointer is on a worksheet tab, a shortcut menu will appear. This menu lets you insert, delete, move, copy, rename worksheets, or select them all.

I Want to Get Rid of This Worksheet

Does your workbook have worksheets you no longer need? Then get rid of them with the nifty Delete Sheet command. Tired of seeing 16 worksheet tabs when you only plan on using one worksheet? Remove the other 15 worksheets and free up memory and system resources.

Start by selecting the worksheet you want to delete. Next, open the Edit menu, and click on Delete Sheet. A dialog box will appear, asking you to confirm the deletion. Click on the OK button, or press **Enter**. The worksheet is deleted, and it won't be back to bother you.

Moving and Copying Worksheets

Here's another Excel scenario for you. What if you want to move a worksheet, or copy a worksheet from one workbook into another? No sweat. Select the worksheet you want to move or copy. Open the Edit menu, and choose Move or Copy Sheet.

The Move or Copy dialog box will appear, as shown in Figure 9.1. To move the worksheet to a different workbook, select the workbook's name from the To

Book drop-down list. In the Before Sheet list box, choose the worksheet you want the selected worksheet moved in front of.

If you want to copy the selected worksheet instead of moving it, click on Create a Copy, or press **Alt+C**, to put an X in the check box. When you're through determining what's moved or copied, select **OK**. The selected worksheet is copied or moved, as specified. Wow.

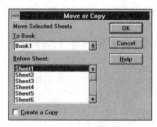

Figure 9.1 The Move or Copy dialog box.

The Old Drag and Drop Routine There's an easier way to copy or move worksheets, and only those of you who read these important tip boxes will know how. First, select the worksheet tab you want to copy or move. To move a worksheet, move the mouse pointer over the selected tab, press and hold the left mouse button, and drag the tab where you want it moved. If you'd rather copy the worksheet, hold down the **Ctrl** key while dragging. When you release the mouse button, the worksheet is copied or moved. You're way ahead of those non-tip-box-readers now.

Name Your Own Worksheet Tabs   When you start Excel, all the worksheets are named with the default name, which happens to be Sheet1, Sheet2, and so on. But you can change this if you want. That's right, take control of the program! Name your own tabs! Select the worksheet whose name you want to change, open the **F**ormat menu, select **Sh**eet, and then **R**ename. Or, you can click the right mouse button on the worksheet's tab and choose Rename. Excel shows you the Rename Sheet dialog box where you can type a new name for the worksheet. When you're finished, click on the **OK** button, or press **Enter**.

Whew! Had enough of this Excel exercise routine? Well, don't towel off yet, I'm going to show you how to start entering data into a worksheet.

Lesson 10

Let's Start Typing Already

So, What Kind of Stuff Do You Put in These Workbooks?

Basically, you want to put *data* into your workbooks. Just what constitutes data? There are many types of data that you can enter into an Excel worksheet. You can type in text, numbers, dates, times, and formulas. All of these things are data. Of course, there are some rules that apply to entering different kinds of data. Don't worry, I'll tell you what they are.

When you enter data into a cell, it immediately appears in that cell and also in the Formula bar up above, as shown in Figure 10.1. Don't forget that. There might be a test later.

Can We Please Type in Some Data?

All right, calm down. To start entering text into a cell, first you have to figure out what cell you want to put it in. So pick a cell. Click on it, or use the keyboard arrow keys to highlight the cell, and then start typing.

You can use any combination of letters or numbers to type into your chosen cell. When you're finished typing, click on the **Enter** button on the Formula bar (the button with a check mark in it), or press the **Enter** key. (You can also just click the next cell to be typed in.) Text is automatically left-aligned, in case you're wondering why everything lines up at the left of your cell. That's all there is to entering data. Or is it?

Cancel button   Enter button   Formula bar

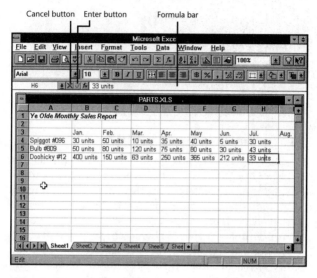

Figure 10.1 *Notice that the data you enter into a cell also appears in the Formula bar.*

Tip

Part of My Text Disappeared! If your text is too lengthy to fit into your cell column width, it might appear to be cut off. Don't panic, it's still there. You just need to widen your column. Select **Fo**rmat **C**olumn **A**utoFit Selection. This command sequence will automatically widen the column to fit your text.

> **Wait! I Changed My Mind!** You can cancel an entry before you've finished. Click on the **Cancel** button in the Formula bar (the button with an **X** in it), or press **Esc**.

Are Your Numbers Valid?

When you're entering numbers as data, you need to know the difference between valid numbers and invalid numbers. (Here come the rules.) Valid numbers include the numeric characters 0–9 and any of these special characters: + – ( ) , $ % . . Perhaps you're wondering why special characters, such as a percentage sign, are recognized as number data. Because you use special characters to write mathematical problems, equations, formulas, and so on. When you enter number values, you can include commas, decimal points, dollar signs, percentage signs, and parentheses.

Although you can include punctuation when you enter numerical values, you may not want to. Why? Because, you can apply formatting that adds punctuation for you. For example, rather than type a column of a hundred dollar amounts including the dollar signs and decimal points, you can type numbers such as 700 and 19.99, and then change the column to Currency format. Excel will change your entries to $700.00 and $19.99, adding your beloved dollar signs where needed. Isn't that exciting? (You'll learn more about this in Lesson 22.)

To enter a number, figure out what cell you want to put it in, then select the cell by clicking on it or using the arrow keys to highlight the cell. Next, type your number in. Numbers are automatically right-aligned when you enter them.

When you've finished typing, click on the **Enter** button (the button with a check mark in it), or press the **Enter** key.

But What If I Want My Numbers to Be Treated Like Text?   What? Oh, you mean using numbers as text, like a zip code, rather than a value. Gotcha. To do this, precede your entry with a single quotation mark ('), as in '04321. The quotation mark is an alignment prefix that tells Excel to treat the following characters as text and left-align them in the cell. Isn't it amazing what one little quotation mark can do?

Hey! Something's Wrong with My Numbers!   If you enter in numbers and it suddenly becomes number signs (######) when you select the **Enter** button, don't worry. The number is okay, it's just that your cell isn't big enough to hold it. You'll have to enlarge your cell. Here's a quick way to do that: use the **F**ormat **C**olumn **A**utoFit Selection command. Highlight the cell, choose the **F**ormat menu, choose **C**olumn, and then choose **A**utoFit Selection. And here's yet another way: just move the mouse pointer up to the column heading and point to the border or edge of the column you need to enlarge. The mouse pointer becomes a double-headed arrow. Now press the left mouse button, and drag the column edge to the width you want it to be.

What About Dates and Times?

Yup, dates and times are data, too, and there's a variety of ways to enter them. I made you a chart to help you out, and I cleverly labeled it Table 10.1. When you enter a date using a format shown in Table 10.1, Excel converts the date into a number that represents the number of days since January 1, 1900. (Good grief!) But you'll never see this number. You'll see a normal date. However, Excel uses the mysterious converted number whenever a calculation involves a date.

Table 10.1   Valid Formats for Dates and Times

Format	Example
MM/DD/YY	4/8/58 or 04/08/58
MMM–YY	Jan–92
DD–MMM–YY	28–Oct–91
DD–MMM	6–Sep
HH:MM	16:50
HH:MM:SS	8:22:59
HH:MM AM/PM	7:45 PM
HH:MM:SS AM/PM	11:45:16 AM
MM/DD/YY HH:MM	11/8/80 4:20
HH:MM MM/DD/YY	4:20 11/18/80

To enter a date or time, figure out what cell you want to put it in, then select the cell by clicking on it or using the arrow keys to highlight the cell. Next, type in your date or time in the format you want it displayed in (see Table 10.1). Click on the **Enter** button (the button with a check mark in it—I keep telling you this, don't I?), or press the **Enter** key. You're all done.

Shall I Use Dashes or Slashes with My Dates?
You can use dashes (–) or slashes (/) when typing dates. Capitalization is not important, since Excel ignores it in this instance. For example, 21 FEB becomes 21–Feb. By the way, FEB 21 also becomes 21–Feb.

As Different As Night and Day Unless you type AM or PM, Excel assumes that you are using a 24-hour military clock. Therefore, 8:20 is assumed to be AM, not PM, unless you type 8:20 PM. Watch out, this is tricky.

Now you know what kinds of data you can put into your worksheets, and how to type it all in. Next, I'm going to show you some top-secret cell-editing techniques.

Lesson 11

Secret Cell Editing Techniques

What's So Secret About Them?

Actually, there's nothing secret about these techniques at all. I just wanted to make sure I had your attention. There is still a lot you need to know about building your workbook, especially how to make changes to your data. That's what this lesson will cover. Are you ready?

Make a Few Changes

After you have entered data into a cell, you may change it at any time. (We like to call this *editing*.) Why make changes? Because that's what you do with computer technology, you use it to make fast changes to important stuff. It's supposed to save you lots of time.

You can quickly make changes to a cell entry by clicking on the cell, which causes the entry to appear in the Formula bar, shown in Figure 11.1. Position the insertion point (that little blinking line where text is entered) in the Formula bar entry (or directly in the cell) with a click of your mouse, and make your change. You can also double-click on a cell to go into Edit mode. If you're using the keyboard, press **F2** to enter the Edit mode in the cell text area. When you're finished with your edit, click on the **Enter** button on the Formula bar, or press **Enter**.

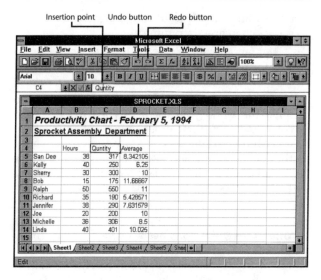

Insertion point   Undo button   Redo button

Figure 11.1 *Make your edits in the Formula bar.*

Oops, I Didn't Mean to Do That Changed your mind about the edit you made? You can cancel changes to a cell before you are done by clicking on the **Cancel** button or pressing **Esc**.

Do-Overs

The great thing about making mistakes with the computer is the ease and speed with which you can fix your little goof-ups. The wonderful Undo command is especially handy. To undo an edit you made, open the Edit menu, and select the Undo command. This will undo your last edit to it's original state before you started changing everything.

Not fast enough? You can also click on the **Undo** button on the Standard toolbar (I pointed it out to you in Figure 11.1). Or, you can press **Ctrl+Z**.

What if you change your mind *again* and want to undo the Undo you just did? Then use the Redo command. (Yes, these programmers have thought of everything.) To undo an Undo (reverse a change), open the Edit menu, and select Redo, or you can click on the **Redo** button in the Standard toolbar. (I pointed this button out for you in Figure 11.1, as well.)

One Time Only! Bad news—there's a catch. The Undo and Redo features only undo or redo the most recent action you took. You have to use them right away.

Fill 'Er Up

Let's say you want to copy existing data into several surrounding cells. Is there an easy way to do that, other than retyping? Of course there is. One way you can copy an existing entry into surrounding cells is by using the Fill feature.

Select the cell whose contents and formatting you want to copy. Next, position the mouse pointer over the cell, press the left mouse button and drag the mouse pointer over all the cells into which you want to copy the cell entry. After the cells are highlighted, release the mouse button.

Now, open the Edit menu, and select Fill. The Fill submenu appears. Select the direction in which you want to copy the entry. For example, if you choose

Right, Excel inserts the entry into the selected cells to the right.

An easier way to fill is to move your mouse pointer on the lower right corner of the cell highlight, or fill handle. The mouse pointer becomes a plus sign when positioned over this corner of the cell. Press the left mouse button, and drag the mouse to highlight the cells into which you want to copy the entry (see Figure 11.2). When you release the mouse button, the contents and formatting of the original cell are copied to the selected cells. A pretty keen technique, if you ask me.

	A	B	C	D	E	F	G
		Book4					
		January	February	March	April	May	Jun
1	**Cowboy Album Inventory**						
2		Quantity	Quantity	Quantity	Quantity	Quantity	Quantity
3							
4	*Title*						
5	Home on the Range						
6	Yipee Yi Yo Yay						
7	Happy Trails						
8	Don't Squat with Your Spurs On						
9	Move Them Little Doggies						
10	Lonesome Cowpokes						
11	Cowpatty Canyon						
12	Dusty Trails						
13	Cactus Carl & The Needlettes						
14	Wagon Train						
15	Chuck Wagon Blues						
16	Rattlesnake Gulch						

Figure 11.2 *I highlighted these cells by grabbing the fill handle and dragging the highlight.*

Secret Cell Editing Technique Number Two: AutoFill

The amazing AutoFill—what is it, why use it? Here's why you use it: unlike Fill, which merely copies an entry to one or more cells, AutoFill copies with logic. What? That's right, I said logic. Let me explain: let's say you want to enter the days of the week (Sunday through Saturday) into your worksheet. If you're using AutoFill, all you have to do is type the first entry (Sunday), and AutoFill inserts the other entries for you.

Type the word **Monday** into a cell. Next, drag the fill handle up, down, left, or right to select six more cells. When you release the mouse button, Excel will insert the remaining days of the week, in order, into the selected cells (see Figure 11.3).

I typed in Monday here.

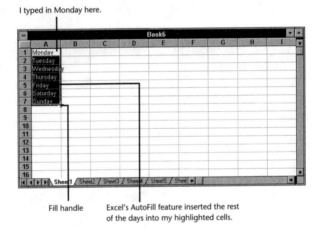

Fill handle   Excel's AutoFill feature inserted the rest
                   of the days into my highlighted cells.

Figure 11.3   AutoFill is used to enter series data.

How does Excel do this? Excel has the *series data* stored as an AutoFill entry. Data that appears in a logical sequence, such as the days of the week, are considered series data. But why let Excel have all the fun? You can store your own series as AutoFill entries. Start by opening the Tools menu and choosing Options.

When the Options dialog box appears, click on the **Custom Lists** tab, as shown in Figure 11.4, to bring the information to the front of the dialog box. Next, click on the Add button. An insertion point appears in the List Entries text box where you can type the entries you want to use for your AutoFill entries (for example, Item1, Item2, and so on). Press **Enter** at the end of each entry. When finished, click on the **OK** button.

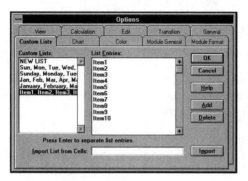

Figure 11.4 *Hey—Look at this! Excel lets you create your own AutoFill series.*

As soon as you've finished adding your own AutoFill entry, you can type any item in your series list and use AutoFill to insert the remaining entries.

Can I Turn Existing Text I've Already Typed into AutoFill Entries? But of course. If you have already typed the entries you want to use for your AutoFill entries, select the text, and then choose **O**ptions from the **T**ools menu. Click on the **Custom Lists** tab, and select the **Im**port button. Excel copies the selected entries from your worksheet and places them in the List **E**ntries text box. Click on **OK**, and you're done!

Lesson 12

Save Your Data, Save Your Life

How Do I Save This Masterpiece?

Save it, save it, save it! Do you have any idea how important it is to save your data? It's crucial! It's imperative! It will save your life! Perhaps I'm being a little too dramatic. But, by golly, this is an important subject. Do you want to know why? Get this: whatever you type into your workbook is stored only in your computer's memory. If you exit Excel, that data will be lost. Yikes! Needless to say, it's pretty important to save your workbook files to disk regularly.

The first time you save a workbook to disk, you'll have to name the file. Pull down the File menu, and select Save. The Save As dialog box will appear (see Figure 12.1). Type a name for your workbook in the File Name text box. You can use any combination of letters or numbers up to eight characters (no spaces), such as SOBORING. Excel will automatically add .XLS to the file name as an extension. The full file name is then SOBORING.XLS.

Hey—Forget About Those Menu Commands, Press the Save Button Instead! For those of you that are always looking for a shortcut, you can also save your documents by selecting the **Save** button on the Standard toolbar. Just click on the button, and the Save As dialog box is displayed (if the file has no name yet). Look in Figure 12.1 to see where the button is.

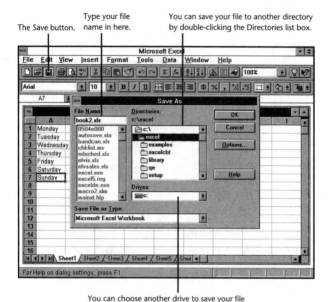

The Save button.

Type your file name in here.

You can save your file to another directory by double-clicking the Directories list box.

You can choose another drive to save your file to by selecting the Drives drop-down list.

Figure 12.1 *The Save As dialog box.*

Maybe you'd like to save your workbook file onto a different drive? To do this, click on the arrow to the right of the Drives drop-down list, and click on the desired drive. Perhaps you'd like to save your workbook file to a different directory? To do this, double-click on that directory in the Directories list box. (You can move up the directory tree by double-clicking on the directory name or drive letter at the top of the tree.) When you're all through with this dialog box, click on OK, or press Enter.

De Fault of De Directory   If you want, you can set up a default directory where Excel will save all your workbook files. Just open the **T**ools menu, and select **O**ptions. Then click on the **General** tab to bring the information to the front of the dialog box. Next, double-click inside the **D**efault File Location text box, and type a complete path to the drive and directory you want to use (the directory must be an existing one). Select **OK** when you're finished.

To save a file you have already saved (and named), simply click on the **Save** button in the Standard toolbar, or press **Shift+F12**. If you want to go the long route, open the File menu, and select Save. Excel automatically saves the workbook (including any changes you entered) without displaying the Save As dialog box.

I'd Like to Give It a New Name

Occasions will arise where you'll want to change an existing workbook but keep the original intact, or you may want to create a new workbook by modifying an existing one. You can do this by saving the workbook under another name or in another directory.

Pull down the File menu, and select Save As. You get the Save As dialog box, just as if you were saving the workbook for the first time. Now here's your chance to give the workbook a new name. Type the new file name over the existing name in the File Name text box. When you're done, click on **OK**, or press **Enter**.

If you'd rather save the file on a different drive or directory, select the drive letter from the Drives list and the directory from the Directories list from the dialog box. If you'd like to save the file in a different format (for example, Lotus 1-2-3 or Quattro Pro), click on the arrow to the right of the Save File as Type dropdown list, and select the desired format.

Watch Out—I'm Backing Up   You can have Excel create a backup copy of each workbook file you save. That way, if anything happens to the original file, you can use the backup copy. Backup copies have the same file name as the original workbook but include the extension .BAK. (That stands for backup, you know.) To turn the backup feature on, click on the **O**ptions button in the Save As dialog box, select Always Create **B**ackup, and click on **OK**.

Let's sum this all up so far. You've typed in some data, you've made some edits, you've saved your work—now what? You've gotta learn how to print it out!

Lesson 13

I Wish I Had This on Paper

Set It Up

First things first; before you print a workbook, you should make sure that the page is set up correctly for printing. Don't grumble at me, it's better to do this now than to mess up your printer later. To do this, open the File menu, and choose Page Setup. The Page Setup dialog box, as shown in Figure 13.1, will appear. There are four dialog box tabs full of options to choose from.

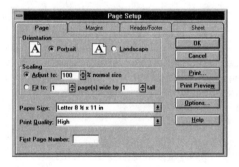

Figure 13.1   The Page Setup dialog box.

Short Cut!   You can quickly access the commands that affect a workbook by clicking on the right mouse button while the mouse pointer is on the workbook's title bar. For example, to check the page setup, right-click on the title bar, and choose **Page Setup**.

Be sure to look at each dialog box tab to see what
setup options are available. Remember: clicking on a
tab name will bring its options to the front of the
dialog box.

When you're done entering your settings, click on
the **OK** button, or press **Enter**.

I Could Use a Break

Here's a bit of information for you: when you print a
workbook, Excel determines the page breaks based on
the paper size, margins, and the selected print area.
(What a smart program.) However, you can determine
your own page breaks, if you want.

First, figure out whether you need to limit the
number of columns or the number of rows on a page.
To limit the number of columns, select a cell that's in
the column to the right of the last column you want
on the page. (Jeepers, this is complicated.) For example, let's say you want Excel to print only columns
A through J on the first page; select a cell in column K.
Move to row one of that column. Next, open the
Insert menu, and choose Page Break. Suddenly, a
dashed line will appear to the left of the selected
column, showing the position of the page break.
Neato.

To limit the number of rows, select a cell in the row
just below the last row you want on the page. For
example, if you want Excel to print only rows 1
through 10 on the first page, select a cell in row 11.
Move to column A of that row. Then, open the Insert
menu, and choose Page Break. A dashed line will
appear above the selected row.

I Don't Want This Page Break After All Make up your mind, will you! To remove a page break, move to the cell that you used to set the page break, open the **I**nsert menu, and choose Remove Page **B**reak. (Were you expecting something more complicated?)

Sneak Preview Time

Okay, you've determined your page setup, print area, and page breaks (if any). Now it's time for a sneak preview of what your worksheet is going to look like before your print it out. Open the File menu, and select Print Preview. Your workbook appears as it will when printed.

You can zoom in on any area of the preview window for a real close-up view of your worksheet. Click on the area with the mouse, or use the Zoom button. When you're finished viewing your master-piece, click on Close to exit. (You can also print from the preview screen by clicking the Print button.)

Yowsa! Another Shortcut Button! You can get there faster by clicking on the **Print Preview** button on the Standard toolbar. I pointed it out for you in Figure 13.2.

Tell Me How to Print Already!

Finally, the moment you've been waiting for—instructions on how to print the darn thing. Open the File menu, and select Print. The Print dialog box appears, as shown in Figure 13.2.

Print button   Print Preview button

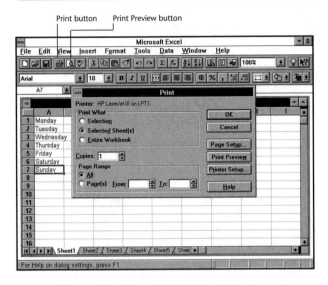

Figure 13.2 *Yipee yi yo, it's the Print dialog box.*

The Print dialog box displays printing options that I have to tell you about.

Print What This option lets you print the currently selected cells, the selected worksheets, or the entire workbook.

Copies Select how many copies you want with this option.

Page Range This will let you print one or more pages. Say, for example, the selected print area will take up 10 pages, and you want to print only pages 1–5, select Page(s), and then type the numbers of the first and last page you want to print in the From and To spin boxes.

When you're through selecting options, click on **OK**, or press **Enter** to print.

Lesson 14

Get Me Outta Here!

When It's Time to Quit and Go Home

When you're done using Excel for Windows, there are several ways you can quit the program. You can:

- ☞ Press **Alt+F4**.
- ☞ Double-click on the **Control-menu box**.
- ☞ Open the File menu, and select Exit.

If you try to exit Excel and you have any unsaved workbooks, a dialog box like the one in Figure 14.1 will appear, prompting you to save them. When you've made your selection, the program will close, and you will be returned to the Microsoft Office program group window. Double-click on the **Control-menu box** to get back to the Program Manager screen.

Why Do I Have to Save? It's very important that you save your work before you exit Excel for Windows—if you ever want to see your worksheet again. As soon as you quit the program, everything you were working on is erased from your computer's temporary memory (RAM). You have to save it to a permanent location, such as your hard disk or a floppy disk, if you want to work on it later.

Figure 14.1 *The very polite Exit dialog box.*

Shortly and sweetly, you learned how to exit Excel for Windows. What a relief, eh? Well don't get settled in, it's time to saddle up and ride the range. (Start the program up again following the directions in Lesson 1.)

Lesson 15

Roaming the Range

Just What Is a Range?

Well, little cowpokes, now that you're working out here in Excel country, there are a few more basics you need to know, such as branding your range. What the heck is a *range*? A range is a rectangular group of connected cells. They can be connected in a column, in a row, or a combination of columns and rows. Connect them how you like, but they always have to form a rectangle. Rectangles—that's what ranges are all about. Take a look at Figure 15.1 to see what I'm talking about.

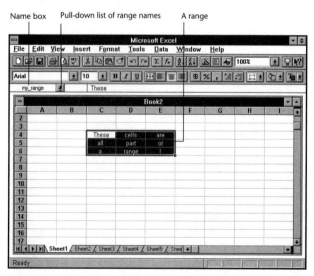

Figure 15.1 *A range is any combination of cells that forms a rectangle.*

You can select a range and use it to format a group of cells with one simple step. You can use a range to print only a selected group of cells. They're also *mighty* handy when you use them with formulas.

Ranges are referred to by their specific anchor points (the top left corner and the lower right corner). For example, the range shown in Figure 15.1 is B3:D5.

Rounding Up a Range

The first thing you need to learn about ranges is how to select them. (This is the fun part, rounding up those cells to make a rectangle.)

Move your mouse pointer to the upper left corner of a range you want to select. Press and hold the left mouse button, then drag the mouse to the lower right corner of the cell range you are selecting. Let go of the mouse button, and your range is selected. If you want to select the same range of cells on more than one worksheet, select the worksheets (see Lesson 9), and then follow the same steps.

Another Shortcut!   You can quickly select a row or a column by clicking on the row number or column letter at the edge of the worksheet. To select the entire worksheet, click on the rectangle above row 1 and left of column A.

Branding Those Little Cell Doggies

Now that you've rounded up a range, you're probably wondering what to do with it, right? Brand it with a name, of course. Up to now, you've referred to cells by their cell addresses, such as B5, F12, and so on. While that's just fine, there's a more convenient way to name cells that would make them more recognizable and easier to work with.

For instance, a column that holds data for the month of January could be named JAN. Then, whenever you refer to that data, you could use the range name instead of the name of each cell location.

With that all said, you're ready to name a cell range. Select the range of cells you want to name. Next, click inside the name box, or reference area (left side of the formula bar, see Figure 15.1). Type a range name, up to 255 characters. Valid names can include letters, numbers, periods, and underlines—NO spaces allowed. Finally, press **Enter**.

You can use the Insert menu to name a range, but it's not nearly as much fun. Select the range, open the Insert menu, and select Name and Define. This will display the Define Name dialog box. Type a name in the Names in Workbook text box, and click on **OK** or press **Enter**. (This dialog box also lets you delete names.)

You'll be able to apply your range knowledge as you begin working with formulas, which you'll be doing in Lesson 19. For now, let's mosey on over to the next lesson.

Lesson 16

Duplicate, Relocate, and Eradicate

Manipulate Your Data

Lesson 16 already! Boy, time flies when you're having fun. Those early lessons introduced you to the basics of the Excel program. Now, it's time to refine your knowledge and apply new skills. It's time to *manipulate* your data. (I hope that's legal in your state.)

This lesson is going to show you how to copy, move, and delete data. All three of these things revolve around the invisible Windows Clipboard. When you copy or move data, a copy of that data is placed in a temporary storage area called the *Clipboard*. You can't see it, but it's there.

What's a Clipboard? Good question. The Clipboard is an area of memory that is accessible to all Windows programs. It's used by all Windows programs to copy or move data from place to place within a program, or between programs. Once you learn to use the Clipboard with Excel, you'll be able to use the same techniques in all Windows programs.

Cloning Your Data

To copy data, first select the range or cell that you want to copy. Then pull down the Edit menu, and select Copy. The contents of the selected cell or cells are copied to the Clipboard. Next, select the first cell in the area where you would like to place the copy. (To copy the data to another worksheet or workbook, change to that worksheet or workbook.) Pull down the Edit menu, and choose Paste. A successful data clone should appear.

Warning! When you're copying or moving data, be very careful when you indicate where the data should be pasted. Excel will paste the data over any existing data in the indicated range.

You can make multiple copies of the same data to several places in the worksheet by repeating the Edit Paste command. Data copied to the Clipboard remains there until you copy or cut something else.

Don't Forget About Those Toolbar Buttons!
When copying and pasting data, you can easily use the **Cut**, **Copy**, and **Paste** buttons on the Standard toolbar. These will bypass the menu routine.

The fastest way to copy is to use the Drag and Drop feature. Select the cells you want to copy, then hold down the **Ctrl** key while dragging the cell selector border (highlight box) where you want the cells copied. When you release the mouse button, the contents are copied to the new location. If you forget to hold down the **Ctrl** key, Excel moves the data rather than copying it.

Pack Up Your Data and Rent a U-Haul, We're Moving

To move data, first select the range or cell that you want to move. Next, pull down the Edit menu, and select Cut. Select the first cell in the area where you would like to place the data. (To move the data to another worksheet, change to that worksheet.) Pull down the Edit menu, and select Paste.

If you'd like a faster way to move data, use the Drag and Drop feature. To move data quickly, select the data to be moved and then drag the cell selector border to the new location.

Hey, There's a Shortcut Menu When cutting, copying, and pasting data, don't forget the shortcut menu. Simply select the cells you want to cut or copy, and then click the right mouse button on the selected cells. Choose commands from the shortcut menu that appears, which includes Cut, Copy, and Paste.

Total Destruction at the Press of a Button

There's something very satisfying about the ability to delete chunks of data whenever and wherever you want. Although erasing is fairly easy, you must decide exactly what you want to erase first.

If you want to erase the contents or formatting of cells only, then the Edit Clear command is for you. With the Clear command, you can remove the data from a cell, or just its formula, formatting, or attached notes. Select the range of cells you want to clear, pull down the Edit menu, and choose Clear. The Clear submenu will appear, as shown in Figure 16.1. Select the desired clear option: All (clears formats, contents, and notes), Formats, Contents, or Notes.

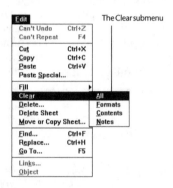

Figure 16.1 Use the Edit Clear command to erase data.

You can quickly clear the contents of cells by selecting the cells and pressing the **Delete** key. Try it sometime, it's like a Houdini trick.

Remember the Alamo! I just wanted to remind you about that shortcut menu again. You can also use it to clear cells. Select the cells to be erased, then click on them with the right mouse button to reveal the menu. Make your selection, and away you go.

I have revealed to you the power to destroy. Use this power wisely. I have also revealed the secrets of copying and moving data. Now that you know how to get rid of some stuff, let's learn how to add some. Look at the next page.

Lesson 17

Add a Few Rows, Toss in Some Columns

Make More Cells

To insert a single cell or a group of cells into an existing workbook, select the cell or cells where you want the new cell or cells inserted. Excel will insert the same number of cells as you select. Pull down the Insert menu, and choose Cells. The Insert dialog box shown in Figure 17.1 appears. Select Shift Cells Right or Shift Cells Down. Click on **OK**, or press **Enter**, and Excel inserts the cell (or cells) and shifts the data in the other cells in the specified direction.

Move Over When you insert cells in the middle of existing data, the other cells will shift to make room, depending on what you're adding and in what direction. If you add to your worksheet formulas that rely on the contents of the cells that got moved over, this could throw off your calculations.

Figure 17.1   The Insert dialog box.

What a Drag Here's another fast shortcut for getting things done. A quick way to insert cells is to hold down the **Shift** key while dragging the fill handle (the little box in the lower right corner of the selected cell). You can drag the fill handle up, down, left, or right to set the position of the new cells.

Building a Structurally Sound Workbook: Inserting Rows and Columns

Not so surprisingly, inserting entire rows or columns is just as easy as inserting cells. First, select a cell. If you're adding columns, they're inserted to the left of the current cell and if you're adding rows, they're inserted above the current cell.

Next, you have to select the number of columns or rows you want to insert. To select columns, drag over the column letters at the top of the worksheet. To select rows, drag over the row numbers. Open the Insert menu and select Rows or Columns. Excel inserts the row or column and shifts the adjacent rows down or adjacent columns right.

Hey—There's a Shortcut Menu To quickly insert rows or columns, select one or more rows or columns, and click on one of them with the right mouse button. Choose **Insert** from the shortcut menu.

Deleting Cells: The Power to Destroy

In the last lesson, you learned how to clear the contents and formatting of selected cells. This technique merely removed what was inside the cells. Now let me show you how to really get rid of the cells themselves.

Select the range of cells you want to delete. Pull down the Edit menu, and choose Delete. When the Delete dialog box appears, select the desired Delete option: Shift Cells Left, Shift Cells Up, Entire Row, or Entire Column.

Deleting Rows and Columns: The Power to Destroy Bigger Stuff

If you think deleting cells was fun, wait till you delete huge columns or rows. Now that's power. Deleting rows and columns is very similar to deleting cells. When you delete a row, the rows below the deleted row move up to fill the space. When you delete a column, the columns to the right shift left.

Are you ready to try it? Click on the row number or column letter of the row or column you want to delete. (You can select more than one row or column by dragging over the row numbers or column letters.) Then pull down the Edit menu, and choose Delete. Excel deletes the row or column.

I can tell by the look on your face that you'd really like to find out how to change your column width and row height next. You're in luck, because Lesson 18 will show you how.

Lesson 18

My Data Won't Fit!

How Do I Make the Data Fit in the Cells?

Grab your mouse and I'll show you. First, move the mouse pointer inside the heading for the row or column. (If you're changing the row height or column width for two or more rows or columns, drag over the headings with the mouse pointer.) Next, move the mouse pointer to one of the borders, as shown in Figure 18.1. (Use the right border to adjust column width or the bottom border to adjust the row height.) The mouse pointer becomes a double-headed arrow when placed on a heading border. Hold down the mouse button, and drag the border to the desired width or height. Release the mouse button, and the row height or column width is adjusted.

Custom-Fit You can quickly make a column as wide as its widest entry by double-clicking on the right border of the column heading. To make a row as tall as its tallest entry, double-click on bottom border of the row heading. To change more than one column or row at a time, drag over the desired row or column headings, and double-click on the bottom-most or right-most heading border. Have you got all that?

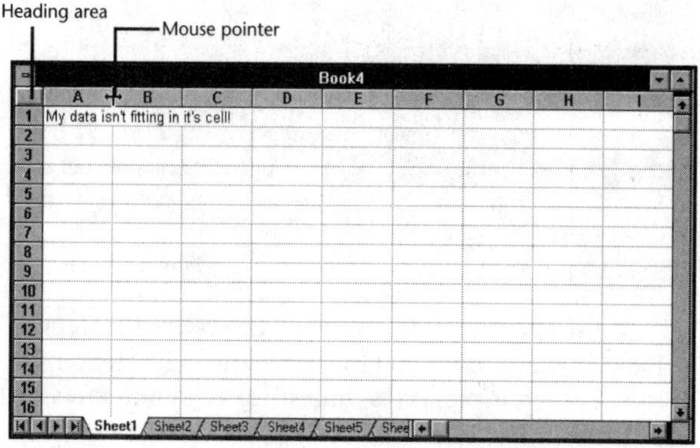

Heading area ────── Mouse pointer

Figure 18.1 *The mouse pointer changes to an arrow when you move it over a border in the row or column heading.*

The Old-Fashioned Way— Using the Format Menu

For those of you that aren't very well-acquainted with your mouse, you can use the Format menu to adjust column width or row height. To change column width, select the column or columns whose width you want to adjust (if you're just changing the width of a single column, you can select any cell in that column).

Next, pull down the Format menu, select Column, and select Width. Type the number of characters you would like for the width. The standard width shown is based on the current default font. When you're finished, click on OK, or press Enter.

The Amazing AutoFit Strikes Again Let Excel figure out how wide your columns should be. Open the Format menu, select Column, and select AutoFit Selection. Excel will make the selected columns as wide as the widest entry.

Adjusting rows is slightly different. By default, Excel makes a row a bit taller than the tallest text in the row. For example, if the tallest text in your row is 10 points tall, Excel will make the row 12.75 points tall.

To use the Format menu to change the row height, first select the row or rows whose height you want to change. (If you're changing the height of a single row, select any cell in that row.) Secondly, pull down the Format menu, select Row, and then Height. Now type the desired height in points. When you're finished, click on OK, or press Enter.

AutoFit to the Rescue Again, make Excel do the work for you. Open the Format menu, select Row, and select AutoFit. Excel will make the selected rows as tall as the tallest entries.

Righto. You've learned to control column width and row height. You're now ready to enter the secret world of spreadsheet formulas. Please take a moment to put on your lab coat and goggles before proceeding to the next lesson.

Lesson 19

Forming Your Own Formulas

Formulas—The Key to Your Excel Chemistry Set

Before we begin concocting our formulas, make sure your lab goggles are securely in place—the formulas you will be working with can be extremely dangerous. Are you ready?

If you've never worked with a spreadsheet program before, let me introduce you to *formulas*. Workbooks use formulas to perform calculations on the data you enter. With formulas, you can perform addition, subtraction, multiplication, and division using the values contained in various cells. All right, so we're not working with noxious chemicals after all—are you disappointed?

Formulas typically consist of one or more cell addresses and/or values and a mathematical operator, such as + (addition), - (subtraction), * (multiplication), or / (division). For example, if you wanted to determine the average of the three values contained in cells A4, B4, and C4, you would use the following formula:

=(A4+B4+C4)/3

Formula Rule Number 1 Every formula must begin with an equal sign (=). It's the law.

Want to see how they work? Figure 19.1 shows the formula described above in action. Table 19.1 lists the mathematical operators you can use to create formulas.

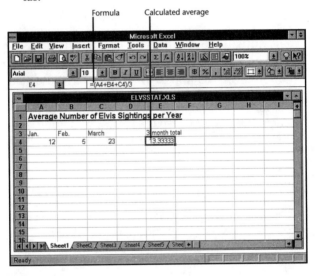

Figure 19.1 *Type a formula in the cell where you want the resulting value to appear.*

Table 19.1   Excel's Mathematical Operators

Operator	Sample	Result Formula
^	=A1^3	Enters the result of raising the value in cell A1 to the third power.
+	=A1+A2	Enters the total of the values in cells A1 and A2.
–	=A1–A2	Subtracts the value in cell A2 from the value in cell A1.
*	=A2*3	Multiplies the value in cell A2 by 3.
/	=A1/50	Divides the value in cell A1 by 50.
	=(A1+A2+A3)/3	Determines the average of the values in cells A1 through A3.

Get Your Operators in Order

You're probably dying to start entering formulas to see what happens. Hold on a second. There's another rule to explain. Here's formula rule number 2: *operator precedence.* Excel performs a series of operations from left to right in the following order, giving some operators *precedence* over others:

1st	Exponential equations
2nd	Multiplication and division
3rd	Addition and subtraction

This is important to keep in mind when you are creating equations, because the order of operations determines the result.

For example, if you want to determine the average of the values in cells A1, B1, and C1, and you enter **=A1+B1+C1/3**, you'll probably get the wrong answer. The value in C1 will be divided by 3, and that result will be added to A1+B1. Why? Because division takes precedence over addition, according to the laws of operator precedence. You have to group your values in parentheses. In our little equation, we want to total A1 through C1 first. To do this we must enclose that group of values in parentheses like so: **=(A1+B1+C1)/3**. This way, Excel knows how to handle the formula.

Just Tell Me How to Put Them in, Will You?

You can enter formulas in either of two ways: by *typing* the formula or by *selecting* cell references. To type a formula, start by selecting the cell in which you want the formula's calculation to appear. Then type the equal sign (=), because it won't be a formula without an equal sign. Next, type the formula. It will appear up in the Formula bar. When you're finished, press **Enter**, and the result is calculated and entered into your selected cell.

To enter a formula by selecting cell references, you must first select the cell you want the formula's result to appear in. Type the equal sign (=). (Remember, the equal sign identifies the data as a formula.) Next, click on the cell whose address you want to appear first in the formula. The cell address appears in the Formula bar. Then type a mathematical operator after the value to indicate the next operation you want to perform. The operator appears in the Formula bar. Continue clicking on cells and typing operators until the formula is complete. When you're finished, press **Enter** to accept the formula or **Esc** to cancel the operation.

Error! If this message appears, make sure that you did not commit one of these common errors: trying to divide by zero or a blank cell, referring to a blank cell, deleting a cell being used in a formula, or using a range name when a single cell address is expected.

Where Did My Formula Go?

After you've typed in your formula, Excel does not display the actual formula in the cell. Instead, Excel displays the result of the calculation. However, you can view the formula by selecting the cell and looking in the Formula bar. If this still makes you uneasy, and you simply must see the formula in the cell, then you'll have to change your cell options.

Open the Tools menu, and choose Options. Click on the **View** tab to bring its information to the front of the dialog box. Click on the Formulas check box, causing an X to appear. This indicates that the option has been turned on. When you're through, click on OK, or press **Enter**.

Display Shortcut Use the keyboard shortcut, **Ctrl+'**, to toggle between viewing formulas or values. Hold down the **Ctrl** key, and press the apostrophe (').

You're now acquainted with the basics of formulas and how to enter them—and you didn't even have to get out your lab coat and protective eyewear. In the next lesson, I'll show you how to edit your formulas. Isn't this a thrill-a-minute?

Lesson 20

Secret Formula Editing Techniques

I Need to Make a Few Changes to My Formulas

Don't worry, editing formulas is the same as editing any entry in Excel. Simplicity is the key. First, select the cell that contains the formula you want to edit (you probably could have figured that out on your own). Position the insertion point in the Formula bar with the mouse, or press **F2** to enter Edit mode. Press ← or → to move the insertion point. Use the **Backspace** key to delete characters to the left, or the **Delete** key to delete characters to the right. Type any additional characters. Click on the **Enter** button on the Formula bar, or press **Enter** to accept your changes. That's all there is to editing formulas.

What If I Want to Copy My Formulas?

That's easy, too. Copying formulas is similar to copying other data in a workbook. First, select the cell that contains the formula you want to copy. Next, pull down the Edit menu, and select Copy, or press **Ctrl+C**. Now select the cell into which you want to copy the formula. To copy the formula to another worksheet or workbook, change to it. Finally, pull down the Edit menu again, and select **Paste**, or press **Ctrl+V**.

In the previous lessons, you encountered the old Drag and Drop feature. Well, it works when you're copying formulas, too. Select the cell that contains the formula you want to copy, and then hold down the **Ctrl** key while dragging the cell selector border where you want the formula copied. When you release the mouse button, the formula is copied to the new location. Pow.

> **Get an Error?** It's possible you might get an error after copying a formula. Verify the cell references in the copied formula. The next section will give you more details about what causes this problem.

Are Your Cells Absolutely Relative and Have You Addressed Them?

Little did you know, but when you copy a formula from one place in the worksheet to another, Excel adjusts the cell references in the formulas relative to their new positions in the worksheet. What's that again? For example, in Figure 20.1, cell B9 contains the formula =B4+B5+B6+B7, which determines the total sales revenue for Fred. If you copy that formula to cell C9 (to determine the total sales revenue for Wilma), Excel would automatically change the formula to =C4+C5+C6+C7.

Sometimes, you may not want the cell references to be adjusted when formulas are copied. That's when *absolute* references become important.

The formula in cells B10, C10, and D10 (Figure 20.1) uses an absolute reference to cell E2, which holds the projected sales for this year. (B10, C10, and D10 divide the sums from row 9 of each column by the contents of cell E2.) If you didn't use an absolute reference when you copied the formula from B10 to

C10, the cell reference would be incorrect, and you would get an error message. (We wouldn't want that to happen, would we?)

Absolute vs. Relative Before you get too confused, let's go over this. An *absolute reference* is a cell reference in a formula that does not change when copied to a new location. Even though the formula changed places, it still refers to the original cell specifications you typed out. On the other hand, a *relative reference* is a cell reference in a formula that is adjusted when the formula is copied. It's allowed to change cell references.

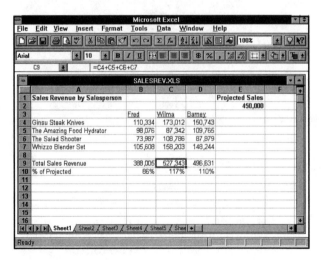

Figure 20.1 Excel adjusts cell references when copying formulas.

Okay, so how do I tell Excel I want the cell reference to be absolute? All you have to do is type a **$** (dollar sign) before the letter and number that make up the cell address. For example, the formula in B10 would read as follows:

=B9/E2

Of course, some formulas use mixed references. For example, the column letter may be an absolute reference and the row number may be a relative reference, as in the formula $A2/2. If you had this formula in cell C2, and you copied it to cell D10, the result would be the formula $A10/2. The row reference (row number) would be adjusted, but not the column. (Is that a bead of sweat on your brow? Steady yourself, you'll get the hang of this.)

Yikes! Mixed References? A reference that is only partially absolute, such as A$2, or $A2 is called a *mixed reference*. When a formula that uses a mixed reference is copied to another cell, only part of the cell reference is adjusted, hence the mixed part of the name.

How Would You Like to Change the Recalculation Setting?

Recalculation setting? Am I going to need a special wrench for this? Yes, we're turning you into an Excel mechanic. It so happens that Excel recalculates the formulas in a worksheet every time you edit a value in a cell. However, on a large worksheet, you may not want Excel to recalculate until you have entered all your changes. So to make it wait, you have to tell it so with the Calculation options.

Open the Tools menu, and choose Options. Click on the Calculation tab to bring its information to the front of the dialog box. Select one of the Calculation options, and then click on **OK**, or press **Enter**. You probably want to know which option to pick, right? Here's what each one does:

- ☞ Automatic is the default setting. It recalculates the entire workbook each time you edit or enter a formula.

- ☞ Automatic Except Tables automatically recalculates everything except formulas in a data table.

- ☞ Manual tells Excel to recalculate only when you say so. To recalculate, you must press **F9**, or choose Tools Options Calculation Calc Now. If you choose **Manual**, you can turn on the Recalculate before Save option.

Well now, that was a blast. In the next lesson, you can learn all about built-in functions. Hey—I saw that, you yawned! Cut it out. You're having fun, darn it.

Lesson 21

Explore the Exciting World of Built-In Functions

What Are Functions?

Functions are complex ready-made formulas that perform a series of operations on a specified *range* of values. For example, to determine the sum of a series of numbers in cells A5 through G5, you can enter the function **=SUM(A5:G5)**, instead of entering +A5+B5+C5+ and so on. Functions can use range references such as C4:F12, range names such as EXPENSES, and/or numerical values such as 585.86.

To qualify as a true function (just ask Emily Post), every function must consist of three elements. Guess what they are. Give up? They must possess an equal sign (=), a function name, and an argument (wow, fighting functions—I told you this was an exciting program). The following descriptions tell what each element does:

- ☛ The = sign indicates that what follows is a function.
- ☛ The **function name** (for example, SUM) indicates the type of operation that will be performed.
- ☛ The **argument**; for example (A3:F11), indicates the cell addresses of the values that the function will act on. The argument is often a range of cells, but it can be much more complex.

And like other data, you can enter functions by typing them in the cells. You can also enter them by using the mystical Function Wizard, as you'll see later in this lesson.

The Awesome AutoSum Tool

One of the most commonly used tasks is that of summing up values entered in your worksheet cells. Because summing up is so popular, Excel created a fast way to do this action. Simply click on the **AutoSum** button in the Standard toolbar. AutoSum guesses what cells you want summed, based on the currently selected cell. If AutoSum selects an incorrect range of cells, you can edit the selection.

To use this wonderful AutoSum function, first select the cell in which you want the sum inserted. Try to choose a cell at the end of a row or column of data. Next, click on the **AutoSum** tool in the Standard toolbar. AutoSum inserts =SUM and the range of the cells to the left of or above the selected cell (see Figure 21.1). If you need to, you can adjust the range of cells by clicking inside the selected cell or the Formula bar, and edit the range. Or you can drag the mouse pointer over the correct range of cells, and click on the **Enter** box in the Formula bar, or press **Enter**. Lo and behold, the total for the selected range is calculated.

The Mystifying Function Wizard

Ladies and gentlemen, we proudly present a new act here at the Excel Paradise Club. Please put your hands together, and welcome the magical *Function Wizard*.

The Function Wizard is a new feature that leads you through the process of inserting a function. Although you can certainly type a function directly into a cell, you'll find the Function Wizard to be much easier to use.

To use it, first select the cell in which you want to insert the function. (The function you have in mind can be by itself or as part of a formula.) Next, open the Insert menu, and choose Function. Or better yet, click on the **Function Wizard** button (the **fx** button) in the Standard toolbar or Formula bar. Magically, before your eyes, The Function Wizard Step 1 of 2 dialog box appears, as shown in Figure 21.2.

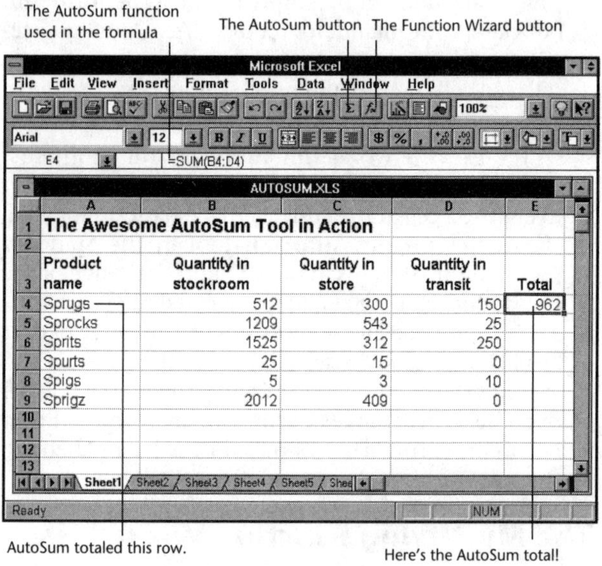

The AutoSum function used in the formula

The AutoSum button   The Function Wizard button

AutoSum totaled this row.

Here's the AutoSum total!

Figure 21.1 *With a touch of a button, AutoSum inserts the SUM function and selects the cells it plans to total.*

Locate the Function Category list, and then select the type of function you want to insert. Excel displays the names of the available functions in the Function Name list. Select the function you want to insert from the Function Name list, and click on the **Next** button. Another dialog box appears, the Step 2 of 2 dialog box. This box is slightly different depending on the function you selected. Figure 21.3 shows the dialog box you'll see if you chose the AVERAGE function. Enter the values or cell ranges for the argument. You can type a value or argument, or you can click on the desired cells with the mouse pointer. (You might have to drag the dialog box's title bar so the dialog box is out of the way.)

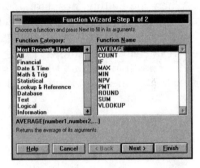

Figure 21.2 *Before you can see the Function Wizard work, you've got to figure out what function you want to use.*

Figure 21.3 *The second step is to enter the values and cell references that make up the argument.*

Click on the Finish button, or press **Enter**. Excel inserts the function and argument in the selected cell and displays the result.

Anytime you need to edit a function using the Function Wizard, select the cell that contains the function you want to edit. (Make sure you're not in Edit mode; that is, the insertion point should not be displayed in the cell.) Next, open the Insert menu, and choose Function, or click on the **Function Wizard** button. When the Editing Step 1 of 1 dialog box appears, make your edits to the function's argument. Click on Finish, or press **Enter** when you're done.

Whew! I can't tell you how drowsy I am. Hopefully, this next lesson will wake us up a little. It's all about making your worksheets look nice, kind of like a workbook decorating course.

Lesson 22

Okay—Now How Do I Make It All Look Nice?

How to Make Your Numbers Attractive

I don't have to tell you that numeric values are usually more than just numbers. They represent dollar values, dates, percentages, or other real values. So, rather than just show plain-old digits on your worksheet, why not indicate what particular value they stand for? If you're working with dollars, let's see some dollar signs! If you're calculating percentages, let's see some percent signs! And how do you do this, you may ask? With formatting, of course. Excel offers a wide range of formats to try.

Once you've decided on a suitable numeric format, it's time to make everything look good. Select the cell or range that contains the values you want to format. Next, pull down the Format menu, and select Cells. The Format Cells dialog box appears. Make sure the Number tab is at the front of the dialog box; click on it.

In the Category list, select the numeric format category you want to use. Excel then displays the formats in that category in the Format Codes list. In the Format Codes list, find and select the format code you want to use. When you've selected one, Excel will show you a sample number of what the format looks like. If you like it, click on **OK**, or press **Enter**.

Ye Olde Toolbar Shortcuts It's about time you got to use the Formatting toolbar! (If you forgot where it is, it's just below the Standard toolbar.) It contains several buttons for selecting a number format, including the following: Currency Style, Percent Style, Comma Style, Increase Decimal, and Decrease Decimal.

What You Need Is an Alignment

By default, Excel automatically aligns data, depending on what kind of data it is. Text is aligned on the left, and numbers are aligned on the right. Text and numbers are initially set at the bottom of the cell. But you can change all that.

Select the cell or range you want to align. To center a title or other text over a range of cells, select the entire range of cells in which you want the text centered, including the cell that contains the text. Pull down the Format menu, and select Cells. When the Format Cells dialog box appears, click on the **Alignment** tab. The alignment options move to the front of the dialog box. After you've selected the options you want, click on **OK**, or press **Enter**.

Use Your Toolbar, Matey! Don't overlook a shortcut like this. A quick way to align text and numbers is to use the alignment buttons in the Formatting toolbar. These buttons let you align the text Left, Right, or Center, or Center Across Columns.

Ditto! You can repeat the alignment format command in another cell, just use the **R**epeat Alignment command from the **E**dit menu, or click on the **Repeat** button in the Standard toolbar.

Change Your Default Format, Why Don't You!

If you're working on a large worksheet, you may not want to stick with the default formatting Excel assigns. Rather than wrestle with changing your data's format to the way you want it to look, it may be more convenient to simply change the default format settings.

You can change the default settings for number format, alignment, and others. Open the Format menu, and choose Style. The Style dialog box appears, as shown in Figure 22.1. In the Style Name list box, select Normal. Next, click on the Modify button. Excel displays the Format Cells dialog box. Click on the tab for the group of format settings you want to change. For example, you can click on Number to change the default numeric formatting. Select the desired format settings, and then click on the **OK** button, or press **Enter**. Excel returns you to the Style dialog box where you can exit by clicking on **OK** or pressing **Enter**.

Figure 22.1 The Style dialog box.

Creating Text Appeal

Perhaps you've noticed that when you type text or numbers, Excel inserts plain text. It looks . . . well, plain. If you're looking for something with pizzazz, it's time to learn about *text attributes*. Attributes are things that make your text stand out, like font style, size, or color. Figure 22.2 shows a worksheet after different attributes have been changed for selected text.

I'll bet you'd like to know more about these text attributes, eh? These are the kinds of attributes you can use:

- ☞ **Font**   Set of characters used for your text, such as System, Roman, and MS Sans Serif.
- ☞ **Font Style**   Includes Bold, Italic, Underline, and Strikeout.
- ☞ **Size**   How big your text is. For example, 10-point, 12-point, 20-point. (There are approximately 72 points in an inch, by the way.)
- ☞ **Color**   Self explanatory. For example, you could use Red, Magenta, and Cyan for your text.

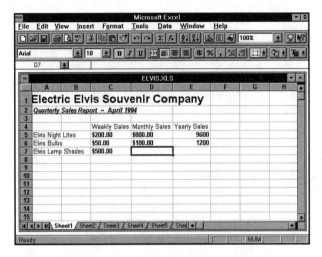

Figure 22.2 *A sampling of several text attributes.*

Text Makeovers

Does your text look drab and boring? Are you ready for a change? Then you need the glamorizing Format Cells dialog box. Simply select the cell or range that contains the text you want to format. Open the Format menu, and choose Cells. (You can also right-click on the selected cells, and choose **Format Cells** from the shortcut menu.) When the dialog box appears, click on the **Font** tab to bring the options to the front. Enter your font preferences, and then click on **OK**, or press **Enter**.

Excel uses a default font to style your text as you type it. To change the default font while in the Format Cells dialog box, enter your font preferences in the Font tab, and then click on the Normal Font option. When you click on the **OK** button or press **Enter**, Excel makes your preferences the default font.

Tip

Keyboard Tip Finally, a shortcut tip for keyboard users! A faster way to change text attributes is to use the keyboard shortcuts. Press **Ctrl+B** for **Bold**; **Ctrl+I** for *Italic*; **Ctrl+U** for <u>Underline</u>; and **Ctrl+5** for ~~Strikethrough~~.

A faster way to enter font changes is to use the buttons and drop-down lists in the Formatting toolbar. Just select the cell or range you want to format, and then choose from the buttons. To change the font or font size, pull down the appropriate drop-down list, and click on the font or size you want. To add an attribute (such as bold or underlining), click on the desired button.

There are more formatting tricks I can show you. You can't say no to me. Turn the page.

Lesson 23

Express Yourself with Snazzy Details

Set It All Off with a Border

In the last lesson, you learned how to make your text and your numbers look attractive. Now you have to worry about other things, like the worksheet itself. Kinda boring, isn't it? I mean, you've got really great-looking text all slapped onto an ugly Excel grid. It's like serving filet mignon on a paper plate. Somehow, it lacks style.

I recommend adding a custom border to set off all of your hard work. Figure 23.1 shows some worksheet data with a border.

To add borders to a cell or range, select the cell or range around which you want a border to appear. Next, open the Format menu, and choose Cells. When the Format Cells dialog box appears, click on the **Border** tab. The Border options jump up front. Select the desired border position, style (thickness), and color for the border. When you're done, click on **OK**, or press **Enter**.

When adding borders to a worksheet, it's a good idea to hide the gridlines to get a better idea of how the borders will print. Open the Tools menu, and select Options. Click on the **View** tab, and select Gridlines to remove the X from the check box and click **OK** or press **Enter**. To prevent gridlines from printing, open the File menu, select Page Setup, click on the **Sheet** tab, and clear the X from the Gridlines check box.

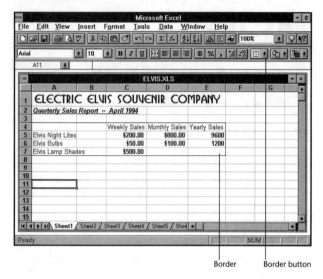

Figure 23.1 Data set off with a border. Isn't it lovely?

Use the Borders Button! To add borders quickly, use the nifty **Borders** button in the Formatting toolbar. Select the cells around which you want the border to appear, and then click on the arrow to the right of the Borders button. Click on the desired border. If you click on the Border button itself (rather than on the arrow), Excel automatically adds a bottom borderline to the selected cells.

Some Shading Can Do Wonders

For a simple but dramatic effect, add shading to your worksheets. Figure 23.2 illustrates the effects that you can create with shading.

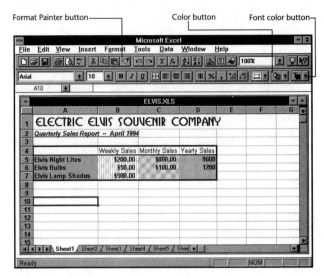

Figure 23.2 *A worksheet with added shading. My, how attractive!*

To add shading to a cell or range, you must first select the cell or cells you want to shade. Then pull down the Format menu, and choose Cells. Click on the **Patterns** tab to bring the shading options to the front. Select the shading color and pattern you would like to use. The Color options let you choose a color for the overall shading. The Patterns options let you select a black-and-white or colored pattern that lies on top of the overall shading. Take a look at a preview of the result displayed in the Sample box. If you're satisfied with the way it looks, click on **OK**, or press **Enter**.

Shady Characters A quick way to add shading (without a pattern) is to use the **Color** button in the Formatting toolbar. Select the cells you want to shade, and then click on the arrow to the right of the Color button (the button that has the bucket on it). Click on the color you want to use. If the shading is dark, consider using the **Font Color** button (just to the right of the Color button) to select a light color for the text.

Other Formatting Tricks

Getting things to look the way you want can be a real pain, sometimes. Excel offers a couple of features that take some of the discomfort out of formatting. The first one is AutoFormat, which provides you with several predesigned table formats that you can apply to a worksheet.

To use AutoFormat, select the worksheet and cells that contain the data you want to format. Then open the Format menu, and choose AutoFormat. The AutoFormat dialog box will appear, as shown in Figure 23.3. In the Table Format list, choose the predesigned format you want to use. When you select a format, Excel shows you what it will look like in the Sample area. Click on the **Options** button to exclude certain elements from the AutoFormat (just choose the formats you want to turn off). When you're finished, click on the **OK** button, or press **Enter**. Excel formats your table to make it look like the one in the Sample area.

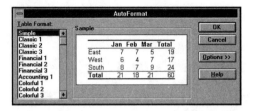

Figure 23.3 *Use the AutoFormat dialog box to select a prefab format.*

The other formatting trick to use is the Format Painter button. The Format Painter lets you quickly copy and paste formats that you have already used in a workbook. It copies formatting specified in one cell to another cell you designate. First, select the cell or cells that contain the formatting you want to copy and paste. Then click on the **Format Painter** button (the one with the paintbrush on it, shown in Figure 23.2) in the Standard toolbar. Excel copies the formatting. When the mouse pointer changes into a paintbrush with a plus on it, drag it over the cells to which you want to apply the copied formatting. When you're finished, release the mouse button. The copied formatting is applied to the selected cells.

Well, now you've completed Lesson 23, and you've learned quite a bit about this new and improved Excel program. You could still learn about charts, however, so keep reading.

Lesson 24

Charting New Territory

Wow—You Can Even Make Charts with This Thing?

The highlight of working with any type of data that involves numbers is compiling your hard work into a chart so you can show everyone else what a math wizard you are. With Excel, you can create various types of charts. A common bar chart is shown in Figure 24.1.

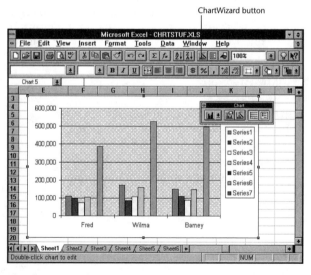

Figure 24.1 *An Excel bar chart.*

Of course, the chart type you choose depends on your data and on how you want to present that data. (That is to say, who are you trying to impress? Your boss, or your client?) Here's a list of the major chart types and their purposes:

Pie Use this chart to show the relationship between parts of a whole. This type of chart is delicious when served warm with a scoop of vanilla ice cream.

Bar Use this chart to compare values at a given point in time.

Column Similar to the Bar chart; use this chart to emphasize the difference between items.

Line Use this chart to emphasize trends and the change of values over time.

Area Similar to the Line chart; use this chart to emphasize the amount of change in values.

Charting Lingo

If you're going to work with charts, you'd better learn the lingo. Familiarize yourself with these charting terms:

Data Series A collection of related data, such as the monthly sales for a single department. A data series is usually a single row or column on the worksheet.

Axis One side of a chart. In a two-dimensional chart, there is an X-axis (horizontal) and a Y-axis (vertical). In a three-dimensional chart, the Z-axis represents the vertical plane, and the X-axis (distance) and Y-axis (width) represent the two sides on the floor of the chart.

Legend   Defines the separate elements of a chart. For example, the legend for a pie chart will show what each piece of the pie represents.

Try the Electrifying ChartWizard

The best part of making charts is that you get to use the electrifying ChartWizard. (You'll find the ChartWizard button in the Standard toolbar.) ChartWizard allows you to create a graph frame on a worksheet. To use the ChartWizard, select the data you want to chart. If you typed names or other labels (for example, Qtr 1, Qtr 2, and so on), and you want them included in the chart, make sure you select them as well.

Next, click on the **ChartWizard** button in the Standard Toolbar. Then move the mouse pointer where you want the upper left corner of the chart to appear in your worksheet. Hold down the mouse button, and drag to define the size and dimensions of the chart. To create a square graph, hold down the **Shift** key as you drag. If you want your chart to exactly fit the borders of the cells it occupies, hold down the **Alt** key as you drag. Once you've got your perimeters, release the mouse button.

The ChartWizard Step 1 of 5 dialog box will appear, asking if the selected range is correct. If it's not, you can correct the range by typing a new range or by dragging the dialog box title bar out of the way, and dragging over the cells you want to chart. If everything's okay, click on the **Next** button. Follow the directions in the dialog boxes to select your options, and click on the **Next** button when you're ready to move to the next dialog box.

When you click on the **Finish** button in the last dialog box, your completed chart will appear on the current worksheet. Whew!

I Don't Like Where My Chart Is, Can I Move It?   Yeah, yeah, yeah. To move an embedded chart, click anywhere in the chart area and drag it to the new location. To change the size of a chart, select the chart, and then drag one of its handles (the black squares that border the chart). Drag a corner handle to change the height and width, or drag a side handle to change only the width.

I Want My Chart on a Separate Worksheet   Select the data you want to chart, and then open the **I**nsert menu, choose **C**hart, and choose **A**s New Sheet. Excel inserts a separate chart worksheet (named Chart 1) to the left of the current worksheet and starts the ChartWizard.

Still Not Satisfied?   If you need to make changes to your chart, select the chart, and then click on the **ChartWizard** tool to redefine the data area and make other changes.

Can I Save and Print This Chart?

Yup. The charts you create are part of your current workbook. To save a chart, simply save the workbook that contains the chart. As for printing your chart, if it's an embedded chart, it will print when you print the worksheet that contains the chart. If you created a chart on a separate worksheet, you can print the chart separately by printing only the chart worksheet.

Peachy. You've charted new territory with this chart stuff. (Yuck, yuck!) Your Excel for Windows education is now complete. Rejoice and be happy; I've run out of things to say. Go and create lovely worksheets. And remember to keep this book by your side (or in your pocket) in case you run into any problems—like forgetting how to use the program, or something like that.

Appendix

Excel for Windows Installation

Have you figured out how to install this new release onto your computer yet? In case you haven't, I'll be happy to help you. Isn't that nice of me?

You will need the disks (or diskettes, if you prefer) that came with the Microsoft Excel for Windows 5.0 package. These are either 3 1/2- or 5 1/4-inch disks (*diskettes* is such a wimpy name) that are labeled Disk 1, Disk 2, and so on. Once you've found the disks, you are ready to begin.

1. If necessary, turn on your computer, and start Windows by typing **win**. (Yeah, the "turning your computer on" part is pretty important, if you ask me.)

2. Place installation disk number 1 in your computer's floppy disk drive (whatever you do, don't call it a "floppy diskette drive," that's majorly wimpy).

3. From the Program Manager screen, click on File, or press **Alt+F**, to display the File menu.

4. Select **Run** (not Flee) from the File menu by clicking on **Run** or pressing **R**. This will display the Run dialog box. (Don't press **L**, or that will make you flee—and you don't want to do that because you're installing the program.)

5. In the Command Line text box type **a:setup** (if you placed the installation disk in drive A:) or **b:setup** (if you placed the disk in drive B:). Then press **Enter**, or click on **OK**. (If you want, you can type **thisisasetup**, but it won't do anything.)

6. When prompted, enter your name and appropriate organization (that's assuming you're organized), and then choose a directory and program group in which to install Excel for Windows. The default directory is C:\EXCEL, and the default program group is Microsoft Office. Unless you have a specific reason to install Word in another directory, you should accept this by clicking on **OK** or pressing **Enter**. To accept Microsoft Office as the program group, click on Continue or press **Enter**.

7. Next the Setup program gives you a choice of three installation options. There used to be four, but the option to **Buy or Lease** was removed because it required a sizable down payment. Select **Typical** by clicking on the corresponding button.

The Setup program will now begin copying the necessary files from the installation disks to your computer's hard disk. All you need to do is follow the instructions on-screen, changing disks when prompted. (If you're really bored, you can read the tips that appear on the screen while you're installing. Or you can try to hypnotize yourself watching the little installation percentage gauge—biofeedback for the computer nerd.)

When the installation is complete, you will return to the Program Manager screen. You are now ready to run Excel for Windows 5.0. There, that wasn't so bad was it? You think they used enough disks with this program? When do you think they'll come out with another release so that you have to do this all over again? Aren't computers just the greatest?

Index